CON FI DEN CE

YOUR SECRET WEAPON

Ashley Korin McLean

A Guide to Building Confidence

The First Edition

DUART
PUBLISHING

Disclaimer

© 2015 by Ashley McLean
Cover/interior design by: **korleyink.com**
Public Relations by: **acmpr.com**
Duart Publishing: Chicago IL. 60615
w: yoursecret-weapon.com
e: cysw@yoursecret-weapon.com

McLean, Ashley Korin, author.
  Confidence, your secret weapon : a guide to building confidence / Ashley Korin McLean. -- The first edition.
    pages cm
    Audience: Ages 13-17.
    LCCN 2015954732
    ISBN 978-0-9861601-0-3
    ISBN 978-0-9861601-2-7
    ISBN 978-0-9861601-1-0

    1. Self-confidence in adolescence--Juvenile literature. 2. Self-esteem in adolescence--Juvenile literature. 3. Goal (Psychology)--Juvenile literature. I. Title.

BF575.S39M395 2015   155.5'191

QBI15-1698

DISCLAIMER

Acknowledgement

To my friends and family, thank you for your love, support and encouragement.

This book is dedicated to my loving Husband who inspires me every day. Thank you for pulling me over the finish line. I love you.

Table of Contents

Introduction

Be humble, for the worst thing in the world
is of the same stuff as you; be confident, for
the stars are of the same stuff as you.
| Nicholai Velimirovic

This book on confidence has been a challenge that I have wanted to accomplish for the past four years. My personal journey from a timid teenager to a confident speaker and author is a story I want to share with others. I also want to provide insight and a useful guide on this transitional journey that one takes to arrive at their confident self.

When trying to piece together this book in my mind, the trouble that I was having was not the composition or finding inspiration, it was the task of expressing my concept of confidence in a way that was relatable to the reader and distinguishable from all of the other confidence or "self-help" books, as most are referred. I have always been a firm believer that if something is worth saying, it should be stated in the best possible way as to resonate strongly.

For me, this is more than just a book; it is a physical testament to how far I have come along in my personal journey of becoming more confident. It also highlights, on a personal level, how much further I have to go. Even those situations that are familiar can still throw you a curve ball and rattle your nerves. The only instance where someone may think that they have reached the proverbial confidence mountaintop is if they have stopped challenging themselves to achieve greater.

There was a time where I would rather run and hide than to speak out, share my opinions with others or even engage in something seemingly as simple as reading aloud in front of a classroom. I can recall in the latter parts of elementary school, when given the task of reading an essay in front of others, I would constantly second guess myself. Although I felt prepared and knowledgeable on the topic, I would allow doubts and uncertainty to creep in, ultimately forcing my confidence to waiver.

For many years I allowed what others thought of me or what they may have thought to dictate my actions, holding me back, denying others the opportunity of knowing who I was and keeping me from gaining close relationships. In my sophomore year in high school, I had the most incredible revelation. I realized that the negative opinions and thoughts I convinced myself that everyone held, were only a figment of my imagination. I was projecting my own negative thoughts of myself onto others and ultimately using that as an excuse to not try as hard, or work as diligently as I should.

It takes a lot of strength and courage to internally look within ourselves and analyze our negative thoughts. When we can be truthful with ourselves and identify the real issues that plague us, only then can we start to plan a real solution that will lead us to become happier and more self-assured in life.

What I would encourage you, the reader, to understand if not anything else, is that confidence is a never ending journey. You will find at times in life you have cleared one obstacle just to turn around and see an even larger obstacle awaits.

Understand that you will never be completely confident in every arena or situation in life; there's always room for growth and improvement. You become confident in small intervals in the same way a baby learns to walk, one tiny step at a time. Also like a baby when they fall, stumble or hurt themselves, we can become traumatized or withdrawn after a bad experience where our confidence is bruised.

How do we hold fast to our confidence in the moments in life that matter most to us? From big moments in life which can include school or work-related presentations or speaking engagements, to our smaller life moments such as the first day of class or an introduction at networking event, it is important to realize your potential and believe in yourself without question. In these moments our confidence is put to the test and with any test, the best results come if you are prepared with your confidence game plan.

The goal of this book is to be simplistic in providing useful tips, tools and strategies that will help you in your big and small moments. With relatable and straight to the point content, it is also my aim to enclose information in this guide that will transcend across an audience of whom vary at different levels on the confidence spectrum.

To close, I hope you, my most gracious audience, are able to receive the message of confidence that I have encoded into this book for you. Please pass it along to others who you think it may help. You can always come back to this guide when you need a reminder or feel as though you are off track.

Best wishes to you!

Confidence is Everything

If you have no confidence in self you are twice defeated in the race of life. With confidence you have won even before you have started.

| Marcus Garvey

What is confidence?

The definition of the word confidence will have a different meaning to different people depending on their experiences in life. Typically, confidence is defined as having assurance in something or someone, while self-confidence is one's overall belief in their abilities and talents. Although often linked, confidence and self-esteem differ in a few ways.

Confidence is the general term we use to describe how we feel about our ability to perform roles, functions and tasks. Self-esteem is how we feel about ourselves; the way we look and think, or whether or not we feel worthy or valued.

Confidence can also be interpreted as the ability to be tenacious and persistent at any task attempted. Confidence is not arrogance or hubris; in comparison, arrogance is having unmerited confidence.

People who constantly brag or exaggerate are usually masking their insecurities and lack of self-confidence. Confidence is something that comes from within and does not have to be voiced. Those possess real confidence do not brag or exaggerate accomplishments.

Confident people typically have, what I like to call, a nonchalant, matter-of-fact confidence, sometimes also referred to as a humble disposition. They rarely concern themselves with negativity or what others may think of them. They possess a strong balance of humility and self-assurance which allow them to embrace their talents and strengths. When one is truly confident, they can admit to mistakes without feeling inferior or as though they are a failure.

Benefits to being confident include:

» Motivational drive and determination to create our own path.

» Helps us to take life altering risks, e.g. changing jobs or careers, moving to a new city, etc.

» Allows us to experience greater levels of mental, internal (spiritual) and physical freedom.

» An armor in battle against opposition and negativity.

» Helps us recognize and respect our abilities and successes.

» Allows us to be comfortable with uncertainty and the unknown.

» Prepares us to handle and overcome mistakes, mishaps or failures.

» Upward mobility in academics and at work.

» Ultimate control over our lives.

CONFIDENCE

Performing a role or completing a task confidently is not about the omission of mistakes. We can often feel less confident when undertaking a new or potentially difficult situation. Mistakes are inevitable, especially when trying something new. One of the most important factors in developing confidence is planning and preparing for the unknown and potentially unfavorable outcomes.

Confident people also know how to inspire and boost confidence in others. This shows in the team dynamic when given the task of working together. In friendships and romantic relationships, being confident is extremely important, allowing you to be yourself with your friend or partner, as well as allowing them to make mistakes and reveal their imperfections at the same time. Confident people tend to communicate more patiently and do not take offense if someone else's opinion differs.

Benefits of confidence.

Confidence is a skill that can help us increase our performance, health, happiness and provide social ease in addition to managing our fears and tackling various challenges in life all while maintaining a positive mental attitude.

There are a wealth of mental, behavioral, relational and internal (spiritual) benefits to having confidence. Being assured in our abilities provides a healthy, well-rounded balance to our lives. Confidence provides mental strength allowing us to feel powerful and free of excessive stress, overwhelming anxiety and unwarranted fears. As a direct result, we gain peace of mind and apply less pressure to ourselves.

Our overall happiness with ourselves increases with our level of confidence. We enjoy health and behavioral benefits such as a better quality of sleep and gaining energy and focus. As we increase our confidence, we become more relaxed, comfortable, and at ease, naturally allowing others around us to also become more at ease.

With a confident disposition, others tend to trust, respect, value, welcome, and cooperate with us more. A strong self-worth allows us to be less concerned with any surrounding negativity including what others may think of us in social situations. The result of a confident demeanor is stronger relationships and more enjoyable social interactions.

When we become free of the mental torment of self-doubt, unreasonable questioning of our abilities and unwarranted criticism, we are able to clearly define our values and realize the feats we are capable of achieving. Internal and spiritual confidence allow us to gain greater insight into who we are on the deepest level, ultimately leading us to define our path and purpose in life. Anything we strive to achieve in life, we first must believe that we are worthy of success.

Understanding our worth in life will enable us to face the future with reassurance that we are not defined by our gender or ethnicity, economic status or geographic location, mishaps or missteps, but by our ability to learn, grow and persevere when faced with challenges. As we tackle many barriers to reach our goals, it is important to have the courage, confidence and conviction to see the journey until the end.

Loss of confidence.

Confidence is lost through a natural need to belong, but feeling unwanted, excluded or undervalued. As social beings, we cannot function without other people. Our sense of belonging dictates our level of confidence while our social systems reinforce our identity.

The attention, recognition, praise, affection and love of others is vital to our endeavors in life, reinforcing who we are and encouraging us to push toward our goals. When the people we care for reject our ideas or undermine our abilities, we are also likely to reject ourselves or abilities. Others act as mirrors which reflect our presence. When this reflection is confusing or does not match with our own self-perception, it can lead to isolation or an identity crisis.

For instance, you are throwing a party to celebrate a recent achievement but your best friend is not only a no-show, but does not give you a courtesy call or valid explanation. This can be viewed as them having a disinterest in your endeavors in life and efforts to grow and excel, and also as a direct rejection of the friendship. In this example, you can actually feel the lack attention, recognition, praise and affection leaving you to speculate the value the other person puts on the relationship. This situation can also leave you to wonder if you did anything to damage the relationship, with their action being a form of retaliation.

CONFIDENCE

When these moments occur in life, it is important to take a step back and analyze the situation and decipher the true culprit of the negative energy we may feel. We should address the issue in a constructive way to allow for a comfortable resolution and follow through on the personal actions we need to take for ourselves to get back on track.

A lack of confidence can show in many ways including behavior, body language, how we speak, etc. It can be self-destructive and often manifests itself as negativity. Without assurance within one's self, we become vulnerable to potential neglect, abuse and allow mistreatment from others. In addition, we also leave ourselves open to a strong likelihood of self-sabotage, which leads to the crippling of our abilities and progression in life.

An example of self-sabotage is to adopt a pessimistic or negative mindset regarding an event such as attending a school dance or working out at a new gym for the first time, even though engaging in this activity could be a very positive and productive experience. It could be a project such as writing a paper or speaking in public, that has a potentially successful outcome, and then allowing the fear of achieving our goal to become an excuse for not engaging in the first place.

When we are not confident, we often lack the ability to stand our ground and defend ourselves against others when dealing with conflict. The reasons why we may fear or experience a strong discomfort when dealing with conflict can be because of previous negative encounters or lack of skill, knowledge, or experience resolving disagreements. In conflict and similar uncomfortable experiences, we tend to be indecisive, second-guess ourselves and hesitant on trusting our judgment.

We must be aware when these types of negative thoughts arise because they often become a downward spiral, reinforcing unrealistic thoughts and damaging beliefs such, *I can't do this*. Replace *I can't do this* with *this may be difficult, but I will try my best*.

Reasons for a lack of confidence include:

» Unrealistic expectations.

» Unhealthy reliance on the approval or judgements of others.

» Fear of uncertainty and change.

» Feeling excessive discomfort of unknown outcomes.

» Fear of a "negative" or unfavorable outcome.

» Fear of inadequacy in the level of performance.

» Negative comparisons and ongoing self-criticism.

» Poor self-image due to a perceived lack of growth or progression in life.

» Allowing past failures and their effects to linger.

» Inferiority complex.

» Problems with issues outside our immediate control.

The confident mindset.

Confidence is a state of mind. One way to nurture a healthy sense of confidence is to adopt a mindset that will promote self-development. Our mindset is related to our beliefs about our ability, which create the mental world in which we live. The confident mindset can help us get through any experience, even the ones that may seem negative at the time.

Confidence is gained by many means. We feel confident when we achieve personal goals that are aligned with our values and beliefs. When we lack confidence, we are indecisive and uncertain, we doubt ourselves. Being able to make a clear choice or decision leads us to gain confidence and develop a strong mindset.

The law of attraction explains that things of similar nature will be attracted to each other. Successful activity will attract more successful activity. This all has to do with our mindsets, how we create them and the behaviors that result. Imagine being stuck at a dead end job but having a strong and powerful urge to find a career that makes you happy and allows you upward mobility and advancement in life. The first step is to visualize and focus time, energy and efforts to attract this new career. This includes working within our network of friends and family to find leads and references as well as finding leads via web listings.

Planning and preparation is a vital instrument in conducting positive and focused change in life, so naturally this would be our next step. If it helps, draw a physical life map starting with the initial desire. This way we can plan accordingly and make the necessary adjustments in our lives to get us closer to this goal.

After planning, we have to consistently implement our plans for our desired career transition. This includes applying for new positions, following up with employers as well as reading and studying materials to help us because successful in this new position. Our will and determination have to be strong and direct; this energy will resonate throughout our journey, leaving an impression on everyone we meet. Remember, the law of attraction is constantly working even if we unaware. Ultimately, the thing we desire becomes ours through hard work, dedication and an unwillingness to take NO as an answer.

While our mindset is heavily influenced by our core beliefs, they are actually built by the simple process of conditioning or repetition, which is the repeated exposure to anything over a period of time, and that includes thinking patterns.

For example, if we had a core belief that *I do not deserve happiness*, then we have unconsciously programmed a limitation that will work against us. The belief that we do not deserve happiness indicates another core position that has to do with self-esteem and our basic perception of ourselves. Such fundamental belief systems are reflected in the mindset which is the basic guideline for our behavior and the daily conduct of our lives.

If we imagine living every day with gratitude, being able to fully appreciate the pleasant and difficult moments in life, then we have adopted a positive viewpoint that allows for limitless possibilities and happiness. For instance, if we have an argument with our best friend, there are two choices we can make. We can develop a negative attitude, while holding on to resentment, harsh self-judgments, which can lead to angry explosive reactions, or we can put positive plays into motion and try to rectify the situation and mend the friendship regardless of where the blame lies.

Negative thinking damages our confidence and can harm our performance. Negative thoughts include fear of the future, fear of accomplishment, constant put-downs, harsh criticism for errors, doubt of abilities, or expectations of failure.

A major problem with this is that negative thoughts tend to appear into our consciousness, do their damage and leave as quickly as they came, with their significance having barely been noticed. We tend to not challenge them and more often than not, they are completely incorrect. However, this does not diminish their harmful effects.

In addition, how we perceive others will directly influence how we are perceived. In general, people want to be accepted, relaxed and free to be themselves, with the absence of judgment. One major benefit of confidence is the way in which others are put at ease when interacting with confident people.

Someone who is genuinely comfortable in being themselves, will project this energy to others. Consequently, this allows others to let their guard down in an attempt to create a genuine interaction, where no one is pretending to be someone they are not.

The self-fulfilling prophecy.

A self-fulfilling prophecy is a prediction that causes itself to become true based on our making the prediction and the beliefs we hold that influence our actions. A sociologist named Robert K. Merton coined this term in 1948 to describe "a false definition of the situation evoking a new behavior which makes the originally false conception come true." In essence, what we believe becomes our reality.

For example, if we predict that we will fail at a task, we ultimately change our behavior for the worst which makes failure more likely to occur. If we believe we will fail, we will not put forth the necessary energy and effort into the project, and it is this action that causes us to fail.

Even when one is extremely skilled and talented, a lack of self-confidence can prevent us from performing at our best when under pressure. The major limitation is not a lack of knowledge or practice but rather the belief that we will not perform well. When we believe that we are good at something, we often do better than when we attempt at something in which we have no confidence.

If one is optimistic and confident, with good thoughts and intentions, good things tend to happen. If one is pessimistic with a lack of confidence and negative thoughts, bad events will be a likely outcome. Such thinking whether positive or negative easily becomes a self-fulfilling prophecy.

Mental Confidence

Intrusive Thoughts

It's hard to fight an enemy who has outposts in your head.
| Sally Kempton

What are intrusive thoughts?

Throughout life everyone experiences moments of embarrassment where we make a mistake, rush to misjudgment or commit a social gaff or error. When these life events do happen, depending on the circumstance or severity of the incident, sometimes we can become fixated on the negative reactions we may receive. Therefore we become plagued, often reliving this unpleasant event in our minds.

Unwanted or intrusive thoughts can be defined as unwelcome, involuntary thoughts, images or unpleasant ideas that are upsetting or distressing, and can be difficult to be free of and manage. Someone who is plagued with unwanted thoughts may question themselves in irrational ways such as, *what's wrong with me, I never catch a break* or worse, *I'm stupid for saying that, I'm never going to make it in life.*

These thoughts are like walking around with a rock inside your shoe. Not only is there constant pain and discomfort, it can cause long-term damage over time. Our minds are vulnerable to negative thoughts causing doubt, worry, anxiety and frequently, it is the same negative thoughts that return over and over.

MENTAL CONFIDENCE

**To decide whether an thought
is warranted or not, reference
these questions below:**

---

1. Is the thought realistic or unrealistic?

---

2. Is the thought productive or counter-
   productive?

---

3. Is the thought neutral or self-defeating?

---

4. Is the thought easy or hard to control?

Tackling intrusive thoughts.

Keep in mind that any form of unwanted thinking which serves no practical value, other than to make us suffer, will constitute negative thinking. Persistent unwanted thoughts can make daily life difficult often taking up a great deal of time and energy, creating difficulties with attention or concentration, and making it more difficult to work, complete school assignments, chores, or just enjoy life. In addition to feeling frustrated or guilty for not being able to control these thoughts, persistent unwanted thoughts may also result in low self-esteem or depression.

While we attempt to rid ourselves of these thoughts, it can seem as though they become more constant and persistent. Intrusive thoughts, also referred to as obsessive thinking, can make us feel like we are not in control of our thoughts or lives. Believing these negative and misleading thoughts only result in anxiety and fear, which allow the cycle to continue.

Overcoming intrusive thoughts takes patience and persistence. We can definitely bring balance to our obsessive thinking and end the anxiety it can bring. Here are some important steps we can take to help us to break the cycle of repetitive, unwanted thoughts:

Identify stressors.

Persistent unwanted thoughts will remain a constant nuisance if we stay connected with the stressors that cause them. These stressors can be people or places that constantly remind us of an unhealthy environment or situation. While some stressors are outside of our control to change, many others can be avoided or eliminated if we identify those things that decrease our energy.

We often do not realize we are under stress until it has begun to consume our thoughts and lives. Prolonged stress can exacerbate health issues such as, physical pain, skin issues, digestive issues, irregular or inadequate sleep, depression/anxiety, heart problems, obesity, autoimmune disorders, etc. It is important to recognize stress before it gets out of control.

MENTAL CONFIDENCE

Stress can negatively affect our mental and emotional health, and create interpersonal and relationship issues. Allowing unnecessary stress into our life can cause negative thoughts to become stronger, causing more disturbance and imbalance.

Try keeping a stress journal. This will allow you to write about your deepest thoughts and feelings while using a combination of affirmations and self-expression. This is a method, tested extensively, that can provide various health and psychological benefits.

Include affirmations in your stress journal. Affirmations are when we "affirm" or use strong words or phrases of encouragement such as *I am solution oriented; all problems are solvable* and *I love challenges; they bring out the best in me*. They include the act of thinking positively about our traits and beliefs which can increase social confidence and self-control, amongst other benefits. We speak more about affirmations in the next chapter covering the topic of self-talk.

A stress journal can also help you to identify the stressor triggers in your life and ways to deal with them. Each time you feel stressed, keep track of it in a journal. As you keep a daily log, you will begin to see patterns and common themes.

MENTAL CONFIDENCE

In the journal write down:

» What caused the stress; make a guess
  if unsure.

» How you felt, both physically and
  emotionally.

» How you acted in response to the
  stressor.

» What you did to make yourself feel
  better while reacting or dealing with the
  stress trigger.

Failure with the first attempts at thought suppression may mean that you have selected a thought that is very difficult to extinguish or re-route. It is helpful to become proficient and skilled at the process eliminating intrusive thoughts before tackling the most stressful thoughts. In order to succeed, we must keep interrupting the thought repetitively. The best method is to start with the easier ones and work up to those most difficult.

Coping mechanisms are learned behavioral patterns we use to cope or deal with stresses, pain, and natural changes that we experience in life. Coping mechanisms can also be described as survival skills. There are negative coping mechanisms and positive coping mechanisms. Many people use their coping mechanisms to benefit them in a positive way. However, we are not always able to cope with the difficulties that we face in life, turning to negative and unhealthy activities to combat these difficult and uncomfortable episodes.

MENTAL CONFIDENCE

**Temporarily coping strategies that
we think may reduce stress, but
usually cause more damage:**

» Abuse of drugs and alcohol, including
use of prescription medication or pills
used to relax or sleep.

» Sleeping too much.

» Lashing out in frustration, anger
outbursts or physical violence on others.

» Overeating or under-eating.

» Procrastination.

» Spending excessive amounts of time in
front of the TV or computer.

» Regularly withdrawing from friends and
family.

MENTAL CONFIDENCE

Although the advice provided in this guide to deal with intrusive thoughts may help some, it does not replace the advice of a physician or other health care provider. If you have thoughts of hurting yourself or others, it is highly recommended that you seek the professional advice of your physician or other health care provider.

MENTAL CONFIDENCE

Focus on the good.

When trying to get our mind off a social gaff or blunder, the natural tendency is to use a focused distraction. Focusing on a pleasant thought or memory will allow the mind to wander on something other than the negative thought. Other ways to distract away from unwanted thoughts can include; playing a game, reading a book, watching a movie, cooking, exercising, or going on a walk. It is also important to focus on an activity that will not lead back to thinking of the intrusive thoughts.

Diverting intrusive thoughts of doubt, worry and anxiety can be a difficult task, but once we make the conscious decision to regulate and filter out negative perceptions, we can better control the expectations we set for ourselves. Negative thoughts become a cycle wherein these thoughts reinforce negative emotions, which in turn can produce negative actions.

For example, if we struggle with pervasive negative thoughts of our body image, these thoughts can force emotions of sadness and depression, leading us to become aggressive and hostile with others or totally withdrawn from those around us. There has to be a daily effort made to program our mind to think positively and expect great things to happen.

When we focus on the good that comes from our mistakes, we ultimately reframe our thinking from labeling those mistakes as failures. Mistakes can be more accurately described as opportunities to learn and grow. It can be said that people generally learn more from mistakes than from their actual successes. With each mistake, we can learn valuable information that can be used for future success.

Positive thinking
+ action.

Positive thinking is progressive thinking; it is a mindset of continuous ideas and unlimited possibilities. Positive thinking highlights our strengths and success, while also giving us the insight to learn from our shortcomings and mistakes. When we dwell on negative past events, we tend to become unhappy, allowing them to generate into bigger issues. Negative thoughts are damaging to confidence and our ability to achieve our goals.

It is important to remember that positive thinking without action is useless. Positive thinking is an excellent technique and should be used regularly, but if one spends all their time self-motivating without taking action to solve the problem, the problem will remain in the same state. Positive thoughts and action are the cornerstones of all our positive progression, and influence the most important things we do in life.

MENTAL CONFIDENCE

How to build positive thought + action.

Observe and learn your strengths and weaknesses.

Write a list of things that you are good at and things that you know need improvement. Discuss your list with friends and family; inevitably they will be able to add to the list. Celebrate and develop your strengths and find ways to improve or manage your weaknesses.

We all make mistakes.

Think of your mistakes as learning opportunities rather than negative events.

Accept compliments and compliment yourself.

When you receive a compliment from somebody else, thank them and ask for more details; what exactly did they like? Recognize your own achievements and celebrate them by rewarding yourself and telling friends and family.

Use constructive criticism as a learning experience.

We all view the world from different perspectives; what works for one person may not work for another. Constructive criticism is intended to help someone improve usually involving both positive and negative commentary. It is simply the opinion of someone else. Be responsive externally and assertive internally when receiving criticism; do not reply in a defensive way or let criticism lower your self-esteem. Listen to the criticism and make sure that you understand what is being said. Use criticism as a way to learn and improve.

Try to stay cheerful and have an overall positive outlook on life.

When voicing a complaint or making a critique, do so in a constructive way. Give insight, strategies or techniques on how the person can grow at a skill or lead them to gain knowledge. Also make an effort to compliment and congratulate others on their success.

Positive thinking must be a repetitive process through which a positive statement is accepted by our subconscious mind, and acting in accordance with those thoughts, they become reality. Success is achieved by those who focus on the good, think positively about themselves and put forth the actions necessary to achieve their goals.

Task:

Identify stressors

INTRUSIVE THOUGHTS EXERCISE

Durations:

5-10 minutes

Preparation:

Pen and sticky pad

Method:

Spend a few moment thinking of the stressors that decrease your energy and deflates your drive. Write each one on a different sticky note. Put all the sticky notes on a mirror and divide them into three categories:

» Things I can't impact or control

» Things I can impact, but can't control

» Things I can impact and control

EXERCISE

Finish:

Repeat this activity whenever a new stressor presents itself. Be sure to categorize the stressor using the guide given and apply the appropriate techniques to eliminate the unwanted thought.

Within each of these categories, prioritize which things exhaust the most energy and confidence to which ones have less impact. This creates a hierarchy of draining activities or people in each category. Pick one of your top three drainers from each of the categories.

Stressors I can impact or control:

Sometimes we are 100% responsible for the activity that is draining us. Our item in this category usually requires a choice to stop or change a bad habit. For this item, write down ways to eliminate this stressor.

Stressors I cannot impact or control:

With the things that we cannot impact in any way, the best decision we can make is to embrace and avoid. We embrace by fully accepting that the stressor exists and will not change, and we are no longer going to attempt to change it. To avoid means that we refuse to allow it to drain our energy.

Again, we can accomplish this by ridding ourselves of that activity or person from our lives. For example, if the nightly news drains you, the choices include stop watching the news or watch it and embrace that we live in a complicated world.

Stressors I can impact, but cannot control:

What can we do to mitigate a major stressor that we cannot control, but may be able to impact? For example how can we handle working with a person who has a judgmental nature or unpleasant disposition? For these scenarios, we can establish boundaries around how we will allow that person to talk to and treat us, for example not accepting when someone takes a loud or hostile tone.

Change Your Self-Talk

Our doubts are traitors, and make us lose
the good we often might win, by fearing to
attempt.
| William Shakespeare

What is self-talk?

Self-confidence stems from believing in our own ability. Therefore, strategies that promote positive thinking and positive statements can be extremely effective. Some people seem to have a natural tendency to think positively, seeing the glass as half full. Others tend to be more pessimistic, dwelling on negatives, on doubts, perpetually seeing the glass as half empty.

Self-talk or our inner dialog is the way our mind speaks to us in all situations, from daily routines to difficult life events. It is the voice that can either encourage us or chastise us. It is important to observe the self-talk we engage in on a daily basis. To have greater control over our confidence level, we must indulge in positive self-talk and counter negative self-talk which adversely affects our performance in life.

The first step toward change is to become more aware of the problem. We often do not realize the negative self-talk taking place in our minds, or how much it affects our life experience. For the most beneficial results, positive self-talk should be used at critical moments such as before an important event or following a mistake. By listening to our inner dialog and shifting it to become more in line with what you really want, we can transform our life.

It is important to identify the situations where negative thoughts and statements typically occur. By recognizing them through prompting at key moments and high pressure situations, we can replace each negative statement we identify with a positive one. Negative self-talk affects us in many ways. It can lead to depression, stagnation, self-pity, and many other negative influences; these combined lead us to not live our lives in the best manner possible.

Examples of negative self- talk:

» "I am not pretty enough."

» "Everyone in my class is smarter than
   me."

» "Because I have a lower income, I am
   not be as successful as everyone else."

When we repeat a negative statement
over and over again we begin to believe
it. When we say *I'm not good enough*, we
may let this affect us by not taking steps
to pursue a goal or complete a task that we
are capable of achieving.

MENTAL CONFIDENCE

As an example, you may not interview for a job that you qualify for because you have already convinced yourself that you are not good enough for that particular position. This becomes like a snowball and affects other areas of your life. Changing to positive statements makes our lives better, and assists us in moving forward to achieve our goals.

Positive self-talk can lead us to live the best life possible. Instead of saying we are not good enough, if we reaffirm with healthy statements such as *I will try my best*, we will be better positioned to achieve our goals. To create positive self-talk, we must look at the various situations throughout our day and in our lives, especially the difficult ones, and change our perspective of them into something that will be positive.

Examples of positive self- talk include:

» "I love and honor my body."

» "I am good student and have the skills necessary to learn and do great things."

» "I will be successful in life regardless of my financial status."

We can catch ourselves engaging in negative self-talk by identifying whether the self-talk is self-defeating and if it causes anger. Negative self-talk can make a situation seem far worse than it is, causing unnecessary stress and potentially more conflict.

MENTAL CONFIDENCE

How to change self-talk.

Observe the way others speak.

At times our peers contribute to the way in which we engage in our self-talk. Surround yourself with like-minded people who are supportive and provide encouragement.

Change negative self-talk with small steps.

Trying to change it all at once can be overwhelming. By breaking it down into phases, we increase the likelihood of making a life-long change.

Use motivational phrases or words.

Write motivational phrases or words on sticky paper and post them in places that you look at every day, like on the bathroom mirror. By looking at these, we will be reminded of our goal and able to use these notes as aids in making our transition to more positive thoughts.

Make a positive-thought list.

Include goals and proactive steps to achieving the positive state of mind you wish to obtain. Whenever you need to shift your inner dialogue, look at the list and remember what you are working toward.

Do not act upon violent negative self-talk.

Please seek help from a licensed medical professional if you feel you may be a danger to yourself or others.

Do not think this is an easy process.

Changing negative self-talk can be challenging, especially if you have been in a depressed or negative frame of mind for an extended period of time.

Do not get overwhelmed or discouraged.

Changing the negative self-talk does take time. Be patient and the changes will happen.

Refuse negative comments.

Refuse to accept negative and non-productive comments from other people. There is never any place for others to arbitrarily speak negatively of us and it is always undeserved. Negative people are a danger not only to themselves, but also to those around them. The challenge with dealing with unhealthy, negative commentary from others is that the interactions with them tend to be draining and unproductive.

No matter what we say, negative people always have an unhelpful opinion to offer. When something positive happens, they are quick to dismiss it as a one-off or point out the black lining to the situation. When they have a problem, they prefer to victimize and complain, rather than work out a solution.

For example, while working on an art project in class, a classmate speaks negatively about your painting skills. In this situation, you must immediately and without hesitation tell yourself that the comment is not valid and is not what you believe.

Although we cannot control what others say to or about us, we definitely can impact and change what we say to and think about ourselves. Dismissing negative comments immediately allows us to replace them with positive feedback. If we allow a negative comment to linger in the mind without taking any action, not only will we begin to internalize the comment, it may also transform itself into negative self-talk and actually begin to affect our performance.

On the other hand, if someone offers us constructive criticism as a means and tool to reflect on ways we can become better at a skill or talent, we should acknowledge their feedback and internalize what we think will work for us.

Surrounding ourselves with individuals that support our endeavors is very important. Negative energy is generated by people that take pleasure in tearing down others. It is extremely difficult to near impossible to achieve great feats with people around us creating a toxic environment. If this is the case, we should seek out other like-minded, positive thinking individuals and dump the old set of negatives Nancys; they will not bring any positive energy our way.

Task:

Affirmations with
breathing meditation

Preparation:

Find a quiet room;
sit in a comfortable
relaxed position

Finish:

Practice affirmation
and positive self-
talk every day.

Duration:

2-5 minutes

EXERCISE

Method:

Sitting in a comfortable relaxed position with
your eyes closed, bring to mind an affirmation
that motivates you. This affirmation should
be one clear statement that makes you feel
more self-assured. Some examples are *I am
a worthy of good things* or *I am just right the
way I am.* Since you are most aware of your
insecurities, choose the affirmation best suited
to correct an inner misconception.

Do a breathing meditation for 2-5 minutes. Breathe easily and evenly, in and out. Silently count each in breath as one count, and each out breath as one count, until you have reach between the 2-5 minute time frame. Listen to your breath as it comes in; listen to your breath as it goes out.

After your breathing meditation, say the affirmation aloud repeatedly. If you are experiencing depression or an episode of low self-esteem, a natural expression of emotion such as crying may help you to become fully engaged in this exercise. Just allow the emotion to be released and continue to practice regularly.

Task:

Visualizations with
breathing meditation

Preparation:

Find a quiet room;
sit in a comfortable
relaxed position

Duration:

2-5 minutes

Finish:

Practice
visualization and
positive self-
talk every day.

EXERCISE

Method:

Increase confidence by using the breathing
meditation technique combined with visualized
images of yourself in a more self-assured
state.

After 2-5 minutes of focused breathing or
sound mantra meditation, such as relaxing
background music, spend at least another 2-5
minutes visualizing yourself at your absolute
most confident state.

If you have never experienced this, use your imagination. Imagine what you look and sound like with more confidence. Imagine others' reactions to you in this confident state.

Allow your imagination to paint the most inviting and positive picture possible. Stay with these images as long as you like until you feel so comfortable with this visualization that you begin to imitate them into your life.

Meditation & Confidence

What lies behind us and what lies before us are tiny matters compared to what lies within us.
| Ralph Waldo Emerson

Meditation has the ability to transform one's self-image, and can be an effective technique to increase self-esteem and confidence. The first way that meditation can boost self-esteem and confidence takes place by the simple act of establishing and enacting this practice. The concept may initially sound a bit strange, but by taking the time to meditate, we are making an investment in ourselves. In turn, this act alone states that we feel as though we have value and worth.

Another important way that the ancient technique of meditation can be used to boost confidence is through the practice of creating a clear mind. Having a clear mind means that we can focus on what is important in life, and what it will take to make us happier, healthier and more productive. Thinking along these lines will help us engage in better decision-making, and this will ultimately lead to increased self-esteem and confidence.

Meditation allows us to calmly operate from a place of power. Many times there is a direct correlation between low self-esteem and nervous energy. If we experience anxiety as a result of a lack of self-confidence, meditation can be used to release anxiety. Affirmations and visualizations are additional techniques that can be applied during meditation to feel more self-assured. With dedication and practice, any anxiety and lack of confidence felt will dissipate and be replaced with a peaceful calm experience.

MENTAL CONFIDENCE

Meditation is...

The term meditation refers to a broad variety of practices that includes techniques designed to promote relaxation of the mind, build internal energy and life force. Meditation is a practice in which an individual trains their minds and thoughts, or induces a strong focus or mode of consciousness, either to realize some internal message or find a balance when dealing with external issues.

People gain a meditative state through practices such as yoga, prayer or spending a few moments in complete silence while focusing on breathing. Some people may meditate on a certain passage of scripture or a quote by someone they admire to fully internalize the meaning and how it relates to their life. Others may focus on a creating a certain sound, or saying words such as "relax" or "peace" over and over again to achieve a feeling of relaxation or peace.

If stress at school or work causes anxiety, tension or worry, meditation can provide a sense of calm, peace and balance that benefits both emotional well-being and overall health. To experience the benefits of meditation, regular practice is necessary. It takes only a few minutes every day. Once implemented into the daily routine, meditation can become the best part of your day.

MENTAL CONFIDENCE

Quiet time...

Establish a quiet time period during different parts of the school or work day that include at least two 2-5 minute sessions. These sessions can be before class or work starts or during a break, where you can sit quietly at your desk and reflect on what has happened during the day. Daily meditation should start with taking a deep breath. Clear the mind by focusing on breathing and use gentle background music through headphones, if possible. When thoughts occur or the mind begins to wonder, as they typically do, we must be aware of our thoughts and only accept positivity.

Task:

Desk Meditation
for practice in
the classroom
or at work.

Preparation:

Sitting straight in
the chair, facing
forward, clasp
hands or let them
rest loosely in
your lap, close
your eyes.

Duration:

2-5 minutes;
at least twice
during the day.

Finish:

Take a final deep
breathe in and
slowly let it out.
Use this method
to meditate daily
or multiple times a
day when needed.

EXERCISE

Method:

Example: Count 1: breathe in; count 2: breathe out, count 3: breathe in, count 4: breathe out.

Breathe easily and evenly, in and out. Listen to your breath as it comes in; listen to your breath as it goes out. Silently count each in breath as one count, and each out breath as one count, until you reach the of 50, or another even number of your choice.

Confident Behavior & Tactics

Body Posture

As is our confidence, so is our capacity.
| William Hazlitt

Confidence and behavior are closely related. Often we can tell a lot about the level of someone's confidence by his or her behavior. Sometimes we can even read a person's level of confidence from the way he/she stands, sits, and walks. Body posture can provide a significant amount of important information on nonverbal communication and emotional cues. In the same way, shy people have habits that force them to act timid and standoffish, confident people have social and personal habits that allow them to behave confidently.

It is firmly established that a large number of body movements, including posture, can influence one's personal attitudes, motivation levels and ability to think. Most people underestimate the power of having a confident posture. A confident stance leads to feelings of confidence. Our posture does not only project our image and mood, but can also greatly affect the way we feel.

Many people who lack self-esteem are instantly recognizable through their body language. Stooped shoulders, concave chest and eyes looking at the ground are symbolic signs of low self-esteem. Ideal posture is when the body is totally aligned with gravity. Poor posture can cause us to feel tired, drained and lackluster as well as cause unnecessary tension that often translates into headaches, shoulder and neck pain, and chronic lower back pain among other things.

Each posture or position we take leaves a certain impression in the viewer's mind. This is why maintaining confident postures and body language will give others the perception that we are confident.

Signs of confidence include:

» Putting your hands at your side or clasping them in front.

» Standing with a straight back.

» Walking with balance and comfortable stride or steps.

Confident people are relaxed, and do not become anxious when interacting with others. They do not bite their fingernails or fidget. This does not mean that people who are not relaxed do not have confidence, but what it does mean is that one cannot feel both confident and anxious at the same time.

Confident people also remain calm and focused when receiving criticism. They do not lose their temper when somebody challenges their competency and sometimes they do not even bother to defend themselves when being criticized.

BEHAVIOR & TACTICS

Clear tone of voice, well-structured phrases, and assertive body language are all clear signs of confidence. Assertiveness is a skill that can be learned that may also help prevent depression. It can also help channel emotions correctly and release suppressed emotions that usually lead to depression or passive aggressiveness.

Art of body posture.

It is said that 60% of communication is in the form of body language, with only 10% resulting in word use. Body posture is important to project confidence from our subtle movements, to the way that we walk into a room. Confident body language sends a direct message to people reassuring them that they may approach us without being intimidated.

Be aware of your body posture in different environments:

» Do you sit up straight at the dinner table?

» Do you slouch or stand upright position?

» How is your body positioned in your usual work meetings or class team meetings?

Benefits of good body posture.

Facilitates proper breathing.

Good posture helps to open the airways, ensuring proper breathing and oxygen flow. Exercises like yoga, pilates and meditation can play a major role in correcting posture and leading attention to sitting positions.

Increases concentration and thinking ability.

When we breathe properly, we also increase our ability to think and process information clearly. Our brain requires a certain amount oxygen to properly complete a job or task. In essence, oxygen is the food of brain needs to produces thoughts and ideas.

Avoid health complications.

A bad posture can result in several physical and health complications over time, such as increased risks of slipped disc, muscular pain, back aches and pain, pressure on the chest and poor blood circulation.

A healthy posture:

» Allows good muscle flexibility because muscles are not over strained.

» Provides normal motion in the joints.

» Keeps bones and joints in the correct alignment.

» Prevents the spine from becoming fixed in abnormal positions.

» Prevents muscle fatigue, allowing the body to use less energy and work more efficiently.

Feel confident in yourself.

Good posture helps us to feel more confident. Try sitting in a bad posture for 30 seconds. Now, switch to a good posture position for 30 seconds. Think of the difference in how you felt. We must condition ourselves to remain in good posture since it is so easy to fall back into bad postures and old habits.

Improve your image.

Maintaining good posture can help us make a good first impression, and enhance our appearance, making us more attractive and confident. It has been said that people with good posture look intelligent, approachable and physically attractive.

On the other hand, people with bad posture may seem unkempt and unhealthy, although they have not yet said or done anything. Someone with a good posture naturally exudes an aura of assertiveness and appeal.

Improve your posture.

Look confident: stand up straight.

In order to look confident in our posture, we should imagine a string attached to the top of our head pulling us up and another pulling down our feet, in order to keep the spine straight, the shoulders relaxed and the chin up. Any time we enter a room we should do a body check; is our body stance straight up and down? If not, take a second and make this correction.

Look approachable: hands by your side.

A lot of us have a tendency to put our hands behind our back, in our pockets or crossed in front. This can make us look standoffish or unapproachable. To find a stance that works, first stand in front of a mirror with arms at your side while standing up straight.

How does this stance look and feel? Try different standing positions until one feels comfortable and appropriate for use.

Look interested: maintain eye contact.

One of the best ways to create attraction is to give attention and thus, value, to another person. A simple way of doing this is to maintain eye contact. Confident people are able to look others straight in the eye and explain a situation in the way they perceive. By looking someone in the eye no matter what is said, the person speaking can more readily be perceived as sincere, genuine and honest.

People who lack confidence tend to avoid direct eye contact, hence seeming 'shifty-eyed'. Do not feel the need to stare at someone; simply maintain eye contact when they are talking. Do not look around the room for other people to talk to or check text messages. It is important for us to keep focus and attention on the person with whom we are speaking.

EYE CONTACT EXERCISE

The purpose of this exercise is to instill the importance of maintaining eye contact. It may also help break through the limitations you may have when communicating with others. It is designed to give you confidence when speaking with others, and feel at ease when expressing your feelings or concerns.

Having this skill may also help when confronting a person by eliminating any intimidation felt through direct eye contact while conversing. Eye contact will also establish the fact that you both are equals communicating on level ground; neither superior nor inferior.

EXERCISE

Task:

With a partner (friend, spouse, or relative) maintain eye contact while engaging in a casual conversation, exchange of opinions or debate.

Duration:

2-5 minutes; optional twice daily

Preparation:

Set a timer between 2-5 minutes

Method:

To start, take even and steady breaths, in and out. While engaged in this exercise, fight the urge to laugh or look away for a prolonged amount of time. If this happens, your partner should stop and try again.

Finish:

After doing the exercise, practice it in the real world. Hopefully with practice, this technique will become the normal and natural way in which you communicate; with confidence, direct interaction and eye contact. This exercise is not designed to teach you to intimidate, but to foster better communication and enhance confidence.

Confidence in Mistakes

I've failed over and over and over again in
my life and that is why I succeed.
| Michael Jordan

Fear of making mistakes can prevent us from trying anything new or moving out of our comfort zone. This is a terrible waste of our skills and talents and can become a barrier to enjoying life. It is a waste of time and energy to agonize over past mishaps that cannot be changed. We need to recognize that mishaps in life do not label us as failures. We can learn something valuable from the situation and move forward.

Many times what we consider to be a mistake is often valuable feedback in disguise. Applying the concept of exploration and discovery, we learn that in taking action to solve a problem, we must explore different strategies. If the actions we take do not produce the desired results, we need to think of various, out of the box solutions to bring us to those desired results.

In using this method, there are no failures or mistakes. As Thomas Edison once said, "I have not failed. I've just found 10,000 ways that won't work." In subscribing with this frame of thinking, we keep a positive mind-set rather than sinking into the negative thoughts of failure.

Setbacks and mistakes are vital in helping us build our success. Mistakes are simply ways in which we learn. This is the success and confidence strategy of the go-getters of the world. After each success experienced, confident people integrate that success into their identity as further evidence that they are unstoppable.

After each "failure", they think about it simply as a function of their behaviors or actions without any personal reflection of who they are as people or the depths of their character. Successful people reinforce their success by congratulating themselves through personal praise. We have to consciously train ourselves to gravitate toward success and allow ourselves to feel satisfaction in our success.

Here is how many successful people think about their mistakes:

» If I make a mistake, it is simply a function of what I did, not a part of who I am.

» What have I learned from the mistake?

» What will I do differently next time?

» How do I adjust my behavior based on what I have learned?

**Here is how many successful people
think about their success:**

» I will make my success a part of who I
am; I am a confident person.

» I will celebrate my success.

» What could I do to achieve even greater
success the next time?

The key to learning from mistakes is
to make consistent corrections based
upon the feedback from others and from
within oneself. When we succeed, we
continually develop ways in which we
can be successful on a larger scale. When
we succeed in life, no matter how big or
small, we should develop the practice of
integrating this success into our identity
thereby continually producing results as a
successful person with confidence.

Mistakes around others.

The majority of people do not notice our mistakes or judge us as much as we think. Fear of what someone may think of us gains us nothing in the grand scheme of building ourselves up. We can never really know what someone else thinks of us; we can only speculate which leads us nowhere. They might be really impressed at our willingness to take a chance and follow our dreams. The only complete control we have is how we think of ourselves.

Some of the most frequent barriers to learning is a lack of confidence or fear of making a mistake. This makes students not want to raise their hand in class for fear of getting a question wrong in front of others. This fear of making a mistake not only applies to their peers but to individual work as well. A fear of getting a low or "bad" mark, or uncertainty about how to complete a task, can fuel a lack of confidence and severely hamper progression.

Once we relax and try our best, we will discover that most people respect us all the more for being comfortable in making and overcoming that mistake. It is not so important what others think of us. It is far more important to understand what we know about ourselves.

Resilience means no half-stepping.

Sometimes many of us reach a checkpoint on our journey to success and fall into a mental block that will not allow us to go beyond and continue along our path. Somehow we get stuck; we become afraid of the success we have worked so hard to achieve. This can typically be interpreted as choosing to stick to the comfort zone or surroundings in which we are accustomed, rather than feel the discomfort and uncertainty of the unknown.

Defined as the ability to recover from or adjust effortlessly to misfortune or change, resilience is a quality that allows us to pick ourselves back up after experiencing hardships or trauma.

It is that ineffable quality that allows some people to be knocked down by life or thrown off course and come back stronger than ever. Rather than letting failure or stagnation overcome and drain their resolve, resilient people find a way to rise from the ashes.

Psychologists have identified some of the factors that make someone resilient. Among them are a positive attitude, optimism, and the ability to regulate emotions, and see failure as a form of helpful feedback. Even after a misfortune, possessing such an outlook, resilient people are able to change course and soldier on.

Once we adopt the belief that mistakes are our gateway to learning and a natural part of the process, our confidence will improve. The confident mindset says to make as many mistakes as possible in order to grow and learn as much as possible.

Get back in the game.

Learning is acquired through a process of continual discovery and refinement of methods through mishaps or the making of mistakes. We adjust our methods until we no longer make the same mistakes. Many people believe making a mistake is shameful and as a result, may suffer from low self-esteem because they never give themselves the chance to develop a new skill or feel accomplished

It can be hard to rebuild confidence after a slip-up. The key is to not let our errors make us afraid to experiment and explore. Once the mistake is behind us, focus on the future. Remember that mistakes are not signs of weakness or ineptitude; recovering from them demonstrates resilience and perseverance.

CONFIDENCE IN MISTAKES EXERCISE

What is the greatest challenge that you have faced and overcome in life?

Think about this challenge as you answer the following questions:

1. The greatest challenge I have overcome:

_____

_____

_____

_____

_____

_____

_____

_____

2. What I have learned from the experience:

_____

_____

_____

_____

_____

_____

3. If not for this particular experience, I would
   not have gained this:

_____

_____

_____

_____

_____

_____

EXERCISE

Plan Your Path

Our goals can only be reached through the vehicle of a plan... there is no other route to success.

| Pablo Picasso

Part of defining our success is planning a path. Planning is mandatory for both personal and business success. If we fail to plan, then we plan to fail. People who plan tend to be more confident and better prepared.

For example, when you plan your outfit the night before, you tend to be more confident for work/school/interview, etc. In lieu of an impending exam, students who study hard and take extra steps such as cue cards, study guides or group study sessions tend to feel more relaxed, answers flow more readily, and they typically receive a grade that reflects all their efforts.

In general, we want to experience the benefits related with the achievement of a certain goal. In our minds, we have a strong association between these benefits and being successful. This association makes success desirable and enjoyable.

By setting goals, engaging in more activities, and exploring more opportunities, we increase our probabilities of success. Personal development and success go hand in hand, making confidence a critical factor in everything we achieve. When we possess a high level of confidence, we are more likely to take risks and try new activities. Success also strongly correlates with the completion of our life plans.

We distinguish certain milestones in our life plan, like graduating, getting a desired job, starting own business or new relationship, and label them a success once these milestones are achieved. Each of these goals brings us positive feelings and emotions knowing that our life plans are being fulfilled and that we are making visible progress.

Confidence Your Secret Weapon

Confidence is in a constant state of change and can be fragile. Therefore, goals need to be reviewed and adjusted on a regular basis to keep us focused and driving in the success lane. By adopting a systematic approach to goal-setting, we increase our chances of success and the frequency with which we experience success.

The only real limitation is the level of assurance we have in our abilities. When we reach the point in which we wholeheartedly believe in ourselves, the barriers in our external world will cease to exist.

Goal setting.

Some levels of success may become impossible to attain without knowing how to set goals and developing skill sets. The purpose of effective goal setting is to achieve what we desire in life in a focused and decisive manner. Personal goal setting helps create a workable plan for achieving success.

Set detailed and attainable goals.

When it comes to completing a task the people who succeed are those who set detailed and specific goals. *I am going to save $20.00 dollars every week* is a much more specific and attainable goal than *I am going to save money.* It is also important to set attainable deadlines that allow for delays and unforeseen setbacks that could easily happen.

An unattainable deadline would be to only allow yourself 20 minutes, during rush hour, to get to a meeting. All your planning and preparation could mean nothing if you arrive an hour late.

Setting precise goals includes dates, times or amounts so that the achievement is measurable. If we do this, we will know exactly when we have achieved the goal, and can take satisfaction from that achievement.

State each goal as a positive statement.

Find the positive alternatives to any negative statement. A positively expressed goal is, *I will deliver this presentation well;* which is a better goal than *I will not forget my script or lines.* It is important to frame goal statements in the way we would like to achieve them, rather than framing them in terms of what we do not want to happen.

Establish a routine, set priorities.

When we have several goals, give each goal a priority. This helps to avoid feeling overwhelmed by having too many goals, and helps to direct our attention to the one most important. It will probably take a few weeks or a couple of months before any changes, such as getting up half an hour early to exercise, become a routine part of life. It takes time for our body and brain to get used to the idea that this new thing we are doing is now part of our regular routine.

Keep operational goals small.

The goals that we work toward should be small and achievable. If a goal is too large, then it can seem we are not making progress. Our daily goals should be derived from larger goals, which allow our smaller and incremental goals to give us more opportunities for reward.

For example, if we set a goal to lose 10 pounds in one month, first we have to break down the number of calories we need to burn every day, which will put us on track to lose a certain number of pounds per week, ultimately allowing us to hit our larger goal. Since situations change over time, it is also important to review goals regularly to ensure they still align with our needs and desires.

Set performance goals, not outcome goals.

Proper implementation of goal-setting requires that we distinguish between performance and outcome goals. An outcome goal is as it sounds, a result. For instance, winning first place in an art contest or scoring the most points in a basketball game are all outcome goals. Performance goals are short-term and personal objectives set for specific duties, tasks or events in our personal and professional lives. They are the means by which the outcome goals will be achieved.

For example, to become the highest ranked student in your grade level, you have to consistently rank in the top percentile in grades, test scores and all other academic endeavors.

Your performance goals will come in the form of individual tasks and smaller steps such as studying for a certain time frame every night, time and project management when completing assignments, as well as attendance and attentiveness while in class. The more we prepare and take the appropriate steps to achieve our performance goals, the more likely we are to achieve our desired outcome.

Set goals over which you have as much control as possible. It can be quite dispiriting to fail to achieve a personal goal for reasons beyond our control. In business, these reasons could be bad business environments or unexpected effects of government policy. In sports, they could include poor judging, bad weather, injury, or just plain bad luck.

By focusing on outcome, our confidence is often based on a comparison with other competitors. It is possible that we initially feel confident, but get completely discouraged when we see the competition. If we base our goals on personal performance, then we maintain control over the achievement, and also receive satisfaction in return.

Realistic goals.

To be realistic, a goal must represent an objective toward which we are both willing to work at, and that is able to work. We only have so much time, energy, interest and aptitude for developing our career paths and completing personal goals. When we set unrealistic targets and are unable to achieve them, we tend to feel discouraged.

People in our lives such as our employers, parents, partners, etc. can attempt to set unrealistic goals for us. They will often do this in ignorance of our own desires and ambitions. It is also possible that we set goals that are too difficult, particularly neglecting to understand the skill level involved or the development needed to achieve this goal. Setting realistic goals is as important as the execution of these goals.

In order to keep our vision realistic, consider the following questions:

» Do you have time to commit to the goal?

» Do you have the education or skill sets to complete the goal? If not, will you be able to learn these skills?

» Do you have the resources available to meet your objectives?

» Do the goals align with your personality and interests?

» Do the goals fit your current lifestyle or the one you are working toward?

» Do your goals complement each other? In other words, does achieving one goal conflict with your attempts to achieve another?

» Are your ambitions achievable in the time frame you have set?

Confidence & goal orientation.

Goal orientation describes the actions we take to achieve our desired outcome and energy we use to focus on a task. Strong goal orientation allows us to analyze the effects of reaching our goal using only the current resources and skills available. Goal orientation and confidence make for a natural complement and combination that enables us to accomplish our outcomes.

Goal oriented people can see the outcome they are trying to achieve clearly and vividly in their mind. When faced with a challenge, they assesses the goal and seek the simplest and most direct path to that goal. Goal oriented people also feel comfortable working independently or competitively to accomplish their goals.

Goals can be either short, mid-range or long-term in nature. Most mid-range and long term goals will have a short-term goal that supersede which reduces the likelihood of becoming overwhelmed or losing sight of our desired outcome.

Long-term goals.

Long-term goals are excellent motivators, where all of the ultimate outcomes we desire become a reality. They allow us to see beyond today and remind us that there is a greater purpose for the time and energy we spend on our daily tasks. Long-term goals can be completed in two or more years. They are the fuel that inspires and helps us to maintain focus while we go through our daily, weekly, monthly and yearly regimens.

Our long-term goals must be clearly defined and visualized. If our goal is to create a successful online business or write a book, then we must detail what achieving this goal entails. We should be specific and visualize having accomplished this goal, as this is a powerful tactic.

Mid-term goals.

Mid-term goals are can be completed in 12 months to 2 years and are important because they allow us to see that our efforts have not been in vain. They further serve as an evaluation tool to chronicle our development and provide validation we are on the right path. By reaching a mid-term goal, we can take satisfaction, relax and be secure in the fact that we are close to our anticipated outcome.

Not setting these goals can result in a lack of focus, becoming unmotivated and even over-concentrating on the long-term goals without focusing on the present.

Short-term goals.

Reaching our main long-term goal requires strategic short-term goal setting. These short term goals can be completed in under 12 months and will help us measure our progress toward our mid-range and long-term goals. They will shape how we plan our time and clarify the value of our time. We should break down our short-term goals by day, week and month, specifically taking daily actions until ultimately the long-term vision has been achieved.

If we should find a daily task related to our short-term goal becomes tedious, we should think about how undertaking this task fits into our goal schema. When we think of daily tasks or short-term goals as choices instead of obligations, we can ease some of the burden and pressure. We know we are in control of our day rather than allowing the task of the day to control us.

On the other hand, if we realize any of the time consuming activities we do have no bearing on reaching our goals, it is time to eliminate or reduce the time we spend on these tasks. If short and mid-range goals are defined then results can be measured, motivation can be maintained and we can concentrate on other life issues; such as health, relationships and other pertinent matters.

Outcomes vs. Goals.

Outcomes and goals are similar yet differ in scope. Goals are typically of a larger magnitude than outcomes. An outcome is what we want to get out of any activity or interaction. A goal is a dream with a specific deadline attached.

When we hang out with friends, our outcome is to have a good time. We typically do not have set goals when casually hanging with friends. My personal goal as an author is to sell a certain number of copies of this book within the next year. These examples show how the magnitude of a goal and an outcome differ.

While outcomes can be much smaller in scope, they are still very important and helpful. By identifying what we want out of any activity or interaction, we will be much more likely to actually fulfill that outcome than if we did something without purpose. If we do not identify what we want to achieve from an interaction or activity, how will we know on what or where to direct our focus? After we decide on our outcome or goal, decide on what it will take to accomplish this task and then commit to plan.

Be S.M.A.R.T.

An outcome is something you desire and/
or want; similar to a goal, yet can be much
smaller. The acronym **S.M.A.R.T.** stands
for: **Specific, Measurable, Achievable,
Realistic and Timely.**

Specific.

Our goals must be clear and well defined.
The more specific the description, the
clearer the path and the better our chances
of accomplishing our goal. Vague or
generalized goals are unhelpful because
they do not provide specific direction. In
the end, it is vital to make the process as
simple as possible to get where we want
to go; this happens by defining precisely
where we want to end up.

Make a specific outcome stating what you will see, hear, feel and experience which will verify that you have undoubtedly achieved a goal. A general outcome would be, *I want to get confidence from this book.* That outcome does not work as well as the following specific outcome, *I want to gain two specific strategies for eliminating my fear of speaking in front of people.*

Measurable.

Measurable does not refer to a timeline; it means determining a way to measure the success in completing a short or long-range goal. An outcome is measurable when we have a clear way to know if we have met our goal or not. An immeasurable outcome is, *I will be confident by the end of the book by using the techniques described in this book.*

Confidence is difficult to measure, so we must get creative and find ways to analyze our progress. A more measurable outcome is, *I will make direct eye contact with people when introducing myself,* or *I will maintain confident posture when initiating conversations.*

Achievable.

To increase our likelihood of success, we must ensure that our outcome is achievable, meaning physically viable for us to accomplish. While remembering we are confident and capable of achieving anything that we desire, we must simultaneously plan a smooth progression, similarly to driving from point A to point B, stretching our comfort zone as we move toward success.

It is important to avoid unnecessary stress and frustration by setting an outcome that is unattainable in the short-term. When we plan our progression, knowing that the small steps will lead to our ultimate goal, we must avoid negative self-thought and be able to reset our goals and achieve higher.

For example, if you are a very shy person, setting a goal to instantly be the life of the party sets you up for failure. You can and will be the life of the party, eventually, but first begin with a small step such as talking to a couple of party patrons and confidently asking questions to learn more about them.

Realistic.

Strive for attainable goals, considering the resources and constraints relative to the situation. Realistic means something that can be done, even if in theory. Realistic outcomes are those based in reality.

Asking for an unrealistic outcome only sets one up for failure. When we set realistic outcomes, we can be proud of ourselves and what we have accomplished.

Before space travel, the average person did not believe or could not understand, in theory, how this could ever happen. Not only have we sent astronauts into space and landed space rovers on Mars, we have gone as far as to land space satellites on asteroids. As long as an outcome has a basis in reality or theoretical feasibility, it is realistic.

BEHAVIOR & TACTICS

Timely.

We must make sure our outcome is timed by attaching a specific deadline to the accomplishment. Often when asked about their dreams, people illuminate with euphoria, and can describe them in perfect detail. When asked what their goals are, short-term and long-term, their tone is usually radically different and do not bear any resemblance to their dreams.

Dreams are what we really want, but those dreams are unlikely to be accomplished unless there is a specific deadline attached with a workable plan on how to achieve them. Goals are dreams with deadlines. Impotent goals do nothing for one's motivation.

That is why it is so important to have an outcome for this book and deadline dictating when you want to achieve your specific outcome with a measurable result. A good example might be, *by the time I finish this book, I will be able to walk up to any stranger and introduce myself.* Another good example is, *I will feel warm and relaxed when talking to strangers in social situations.*

Goal setting is the powerful process of thinking about our ideal future, combined with the motivation we need to turn the vision of this future into reality. It is an important technique used by top level business professionals, scholars, athletes and achievers in all fields. It focuses our acquisition of knowledge, and helps us to organize our time and resources so that we can make the most of life.

By setting sharp, clearly defined goals, we can measure and take pride in the achievement of those goals, and see forward progress in what might previously have seemed like a long pointless grind. This will also raise confidence, as we recognize our abilities and competence in achieving the goals set.

Success comes to those that plan.

The process of setting goals helps us choose and map out where we want to go in life. During this process, we can also quickly spot the distractions that can lead us astray. By knowing precisely what we want to achieve, we know where to concentrate our efforts.

Perhaps one of the most immediate effects of goal setting is the gratification we feel when we set a goal, stick to a plan, and achieve it. We have to reach a goal only once to know that the fulfillment and pleasure we derive. Achieving a goal is a strong catalyst for returning to, and relying on, strong goal-setting techniques and methods.

Goal setting keeps us focused on our chosen direction and acts as a reference point any time we feel we have strayed from our path. In this capacity, goal setting offers yet another benefit, which is to help us more identify the distractions that are roadblocks on our path to success and happiness.

Visions & Goals

Visualize your life in 1, 5 & 10 years. Think about what you see, hear, and feel in your ideal life. Who is there? How do you spend your time? Where do you spend your time?

For each chart list 3 goals you want to achieve pertaining to your personal life, health and career. Also provide a timeline as to when you want to have this goal accomplished.

EXERCISE

What is your 10 yr. Goal:

EXERCISE

PERSONAL

HEALTH

CAREER

Timeline (by when):

EXERCISE

What is your 5 yr. Goal:

EXERCISE

PERSONAL	

HEALTH	

CAREER	

Timeline (by when):

EXERCISE

What is your 1 yr. Goal:

EXERCISE

PERSONAL	
HEALTH	
CAREER	

Timeline (by when):

EXERCISE

**PLAN YOUR
PATH
EXERCISE 2**

EXERCISE

1. Write down one of your 5 yr. goals from exercise 1. My goal is to:

_____

_____

_____

_____

_____

_____

_____

_____

2. Make your goal detailed and **SPECIFIC**.
(Answer who/what/where/how/when):

_____

_____

_____

_____

_____

_____

_____

_____

_____

_____

_____

_____

3. Why is this goal meaningful for you?

_____

_____

_____

_____

_____

_____

_____

_____

_____

_____

_____

_____

_____

_____

EXERCISE

4. HOW will you reach this goal? List at least 3 action steps you will take (be specific):

_____

_____

_____

_____

_____

_____

_____

_____

_____

_____

_____

5. Make your goal **MEASURABLE**. Add measurements and tracking details.

» I will measure/track my goal by using the following methods:

_____

_____

_____

_____

_____

_____

_____

_____

_____

_____

_____

_____

EXERCISE

» I will know I've reached my goal when:

_____

_____

_____

_____

_____

_____

_____

_____

_____

_____

_____

_____

_____

EXERCISE

6. Make your goal **ATTAINABLE**. What additional resources do you need for success?

» Items I need to achieve this goal:

_____

_____

_____

_____

_____

_____

_____

_____

_____

_____

_____

_____

EXERCISE

» How will I find the time:

_____

_____

_____

_____

_____

_____

_____

_____

_____

_____

_____

_____

_____

» Things I need to learn more about:

_____

_____

_____

_____

_____

_____

_____

» People I can talk to for support:

_____

_____

_____

_____

_____

_____

_____

7. What is a realistic outcome for your goal?

_____

_____

_____

_____

_____

_____

_____

_____

_____

_____

_____

_____

_____

_____

8. Make your goal **TIMELY**. Put a deadline on your goal and set some benchmarks.

» I will reach my goal by (date):

___/___/____.

» My halfway point (or checkpoint) or measurement will be _____ _____ on (date) ___/___/____.

» Additional dates and milestones I will aim for:

_____

_____

_____

_____

_____

_____

_____

EXERCISE

Confident Relations
& Remedies

Identify Your Support System

Keep away from people who try to belittle your ambitions. Small people always do that but the really great ones make you feel that you too can become great.
| Mark Twain

General studies have shown that a significant part of our self-concept is based upon our social identity. Our social identity is related to our beliefs concerning the groups with which we affiliate. A strong social support system is critical for teens and adults alike to maximize our potential and achieve our goals.

It will determine how well we build and maintain the self-confidence necessary for success. Social support is an important factor in developing and maintaining healthy lifestyle behaviors. They can play a protective role in helping to reduce stress and provide support and encouragement for our goals and plans.

When establishing a support system, it is also important to focus on what we can give to others. When we think about support systems, we may think about surrounding ourselves with people who will offer us support and guidance. However, if we focus too heavily on that aspect of the relationship, others may find that our friendship is too burdensome, and our friends may not have the energy or desire to keep giving.

When we give of ourselves to our friends and family, and stay mindful of their needs, we experience joy and a deeper connection to that person. We help them become a stronger person who is more readily prepared to help us in our time of need.

Guidelines to building a strong support system.

The golden rule.

When building a support system with those whom we spend the bulk of our time, remember, everyone invited into our life should help us to become a better person. Hang only with people who support your quest to be great or they must go away.

Unconditional love.

No man is an island; meaning we all need people to achieve and be successful, and cannot thrive through life on our own. When we have a support system that loves us unconditionally, they are happy without reservation when we succeed and celebrate as if the success belongs to them.

They give us constructive criticism when we make a mistake or flat out screw-up, and will continue to support us in becoming better. The mere presence of these people in life builds self-confidence because of the genuine support and care they bring.

No 'HATAS' allowed.

Disgruntled and negative people, if they were not so dangerous, could be considered pitiable. They are miserable people who have already concluded that they do not have the talent, drive or intellect to be successful. Haters are the polar opposite of those who bring unconditional love to our lives. Rather than rejoicing in the success of others, haters revel in the misfortune of others.

Haters plot and scheme in the hopes of sabotaging any attempt one makes to be great. They arc the biggest threat to self-confidence and should be avoided at all costs. Find ways to use these negative people as additional motivation and not reason to fail.

Compete with self, not others.

A benefit of having a solid support system is the comfort and security of being able to expose one's weakness without fear of undeserved commentary or negative reactions. When someone considers themselves to be in direct competition with us, and becomes privy to this weakness, it is a natural reaction, on their part, to use this to their own advantage. Anyone seeking the same prize or position as us, will view us as competition and therefore, should not be in our support system except under the rarest of circumstances.

No "Yes" men or women.

"Yes" men or enablers are people that only tell others want they want to hear, never giving any credible or well-thought out advice. Even worse is that the advice they give always seems to result in more trouble and greater woes. Enablers are the ones that talk us into going out to party the night before a big test or convince us to have that extra piece of cake when we are on a diet.

In some ways, enablers are the most difficult of the negative influences to spot because their behavior appears to be unconditional love. We must be extra vigilant to ensure that enablers do not drag us into something that we know we should be avoiding.

First, be a friend to yourself.

Anyone who wants others to do well will start by putting themselves in the best position to succeed. Great leaders work to create an environment for others that is conducive to success. Similarly, being your own best friend means accepting the challenge of being great while working diligently to achieve personal success.

How do you become a better friend to yourself? Take every opportunity to learn more about yourself and use this knowledge to perform at your best under the most favorable circumstances possible. For example, if you are a morning person, schedule study times and other activities during this part of the day; during other parts of the day, you may not be able to do your best work.

With support,
we flourish.

Having multiple levels of support from different people is also very important. If a support system is limited to only one person, we risk the chance of wearing that one person out, stretching them too thin, or feeling unsupported if that person is unavailable. It is always better for everyone if a support system has at least a few people on which we can depend. We can look for support networks at home, work, school, church, etc.

A strong support network will celebrate our strengths and help us to overcome our weaknesses. They will also help us frame the situations that we are going through in a constructive light. Support systems can also teach us what it means to be part of a something larger than ourselves.

1. Write down the name of one person who genuinely adores you and that you would like to spend more time with:

_____

_____

_____

_____

_____

_____

_____

2. Pick up the phone today, schedule a time to get together and be sure to talk with this person about getting together on a regular basis:

_____

_____

_____

_____

_____

EXERCISE

3. Write down the name of one person who is great at speaking the truth with love to you. It has to be someone who cares enough to help you see yourself clearly:

_____

_____

_____

_____

_____

4. If you have no one who plays this role in your life, how might you go about creating this type of friendship?

_____

_____

_____

_____

_____

_____

_____

_____

_____

_____

_____

_____

EXERCISE

5. Pick up the phone today, schedule a time to get together and be sure to talk with this person about getting together on a regular basis:

_____

_____

_____

_____

_____

6. Write down the name of one person who is great at "speaking the truth with love" to you. It has to be someone who cares enough to help you see yourself clearly:

_____

_____

_____

_____

_____

7. If you have no one who plays this role in your life, how might you go about creating this type of friendship?

_____

_____

_____

_____

_____

_____

_____

_____

_____

_____

_____

_____

_____

8. Name one person in your life to whom you would like to show greater support. How will you go about showing this person that you care about and believe in him or her?

_____

_____

_____

_____

_____

_____

_____

_____

Confidence Your Secret Weapon

Dealing with Conflict

In conflict, be fair and generous.
| Tao Te Ching

Conflict happens from the classroom to the corporate board room and everywhere in between. Some form of disagreement is often considered to be a normal and healthy part of a relationship. No two people will agree on everything at all time. By learning skills needed for successful conflict resolution, we can keep our personal and professional relationships strong and growing.

Conflicts arise when people disagree over their values, motivations, perceptions, ideas, or desires. Sometimes these differences may appear trivial, but when a conflict triggers a strong feeling or repressed emotion such as anger or depression, a deep personal and relational need is at the core of the problem. This internal need can be to feel respected and valued, safe and secure or to be understood or recognized.

For example, think of the transition process from an emotionally attached child to a, sometimes, distant, moody, or rebellious teenager to be a normal stage of development. As adolescents begin to find their identities, interest and support system of friends, they can begin to pull away from the safety of family and assert their independence as they start their journey into adulthood.

It is normal for any person, especially adolescents, to disagree or have a conflict with parents, friends or family members. Because adolescents are going through physical and emotional changes, it is normal that at times they may feel an inadequacy in themselves, their skill sets or the relationships they have with others. These internal confusions and sensitivities can lead them to conflicts that an adult would be able to defuse or navigate around altogether.

Ongoing conflict can be stressful and damaging to relationships. Some people find it difficult to manage their feelings and become intentionally hurtful, aggressive or even violent. Sometimes, strong emotions or the power imbalances that can be present in relationships are difficult to resolve and can only be addressed in a counseling session.

Conflicts are inevitable and learning to deal with them in a healthy way is vital. When conflict is mismanaged, it can harm the relationship, but when handled in a respectful and positive way, conflict provides an opportunity for growth, ultimately strengthening the bond between two people.

Confidence & conflict.

Conflict can occur when our views or beliefs clash with those of friends or family members, or a simple misunderstanding can cause the parties involved to jump to the wrong conclusion. Issues of conflict that are not resolved peacefully can lead to arguments and resentment.

Many people try to avoid conflict simply because they do not feel adequately equipped to address an issue. Like many fears, the fear of conflict is primarily based on our thoughts and presumptions. We fear the reaction of others, and how those reactions may or may not make us feel.

A fear of conflict will also discourage us from providing insightful feedback, comments, constructive criticism, or asking questions because we think the other person will feel uncomfortable or hurt, or worse, we receive a negative reaction or open the door for a conflict.

Whether it is in our family, social or academic life, avoiding conflicts does not serve us well. In reality, we short change ourselves. Conflict avoidance can lead us to becoming a person who is easily pushed around (a 'pushover'), 'yes man' (or 'yes women') or someone with a lot of buried anger and frustration. It is healthy and necessary to address the situations we avoid because of fear of conflict.

Agreeing to negotiate.

Typically, our first impulse is anger. We tend to push the point that we are right, our opponent is wrong and attempt to win the argument at any cost. Finding a peaceful resolution can be difficult, if not impossible, when both parties stubbornly stick to their guns. It helps if the parties involved decide collectively to listen to each other and negotiate a resolution instead.

Open and honest communication is a positive way we can help reduce conflict so that disagreements with friends and family members can reach a peaceful resolution. This usually means that everyone agrees to a compromise or agrees to disagree.

Some suggestions to conflict resolution include:

» Decide if the issue is worth fighting over.

» Define the problem and stick to the topic.

» Separate the problem or issue from the actual person.

» Cool off and calm down first if you feel too angry to talk calmly.

» Keep in mind that the idea is to resolve the conflict, not win the argument.

» Remember that the other party is not obliged to always agree with you.

» Respect the other person's point of view.

» Talk clearly and reasonably.

» Try to find points of common ground.

» If all else fails, agree to disagree.

Overcoming the fear of conflict with confidence.

People who are confident do not have a fear of conflict because they do not approach the situation assuming that it will turn into a confrontation. Rather, we should approach situations prepared to clearly articulate and communicate the issue while remaining calm and confident. Confident people do not lose their cool, make anyone feel insecure, threatened or inadequate. This links back to confident people knowing who they are, being comfortable and secure with who they are, and standing firmly on their morals.

RELATIONS & REMEDIES

Confident people do not paint the worst outcome in their minds all the time. They visualize and plant positive seeds and normally, those tend to be the type of outcomes they receive. As we put the time and effort into developing our self-confidence, we will begin to notice our fear of conflict melt away.

Understanding that a conflict is not the end of the world but rather a slight misunderstanding or disagreement will go a long way. Ultimately, a "conflict" is a situation where a conversation needs to take place and a resolution needs to be implemented.

Steps to conflict resolution.

Take a breathe deep, remain calm.

Compose yourself before trying to resolve the situation. Try not to overreact. By remaining calm it is more likely that the other person will consider our viewpoint. Conflicts cannot be solved when we are hot under the collar and our words are emotionally loaded. Choose your response rather than just giving a reaction.

It is also important to remain calm so that we are able to hold on to our thoughts and not clam up because we are nervous. When one person becomes silent and stops responding to the other, frustration and anger can result. Positive results can only be attained through two-way communication.

RELATIONS & REMEDIES

Inform the other person of your position.

Make a strong attempt to be clear about your stance on the issue and avoid vague complaints. Explaining to someone directly and honestly how you feel is a very powerful form of communication. If you start to feel so angry or upset that you feel as though you may lose control, take a time out and do something to help your revert back to your calm and relaxed state.

Another way to accomplish this task is through the "I statements" exercise, which is a tool for expressing how we feel without attacking or blaming. By starting from "I" we take responsibility for the way we perceive the problem. "You messages" put others on the defensive and close doors to communication.

For example, a statement like, *"You did not put gas in the car after you used it! Why do you always do that?"* will escalate the conflict. Using an "I" message comes such as *"I'm disappointed because we agreed you would put some gas in the car after each use. What happened?"* will make them less defensive.

Agree to try to work together to find a solution peacefully, and establish ground rules. For example, no name-calling, blaming, yelling, or interrupting. Personal attacks create an atmosphere of distrust, anger, and vulnerability and making accusations will back the other person into a corner, forcing them to defend themselves.

Each person describes the dispute from his or her perspective, without interruption.

The person listening should pay close attention, then ask questions to clarify any concerns. The listener should not only consider what the other participant is saying or what they want, but also why they want it.

For example, if someone insists that you pay for something they believe you broke, misplaced, etc., they may be doing so not because they genuinely care about the object or the replacement money, but because they feel disrespected or unappreciated.

Addressing the issue of the other person's need to feel respected may be needed in order to resolve the conflict. Reflective listening demonstrates that we care enough to hear the other person out, rather than just focusing on our own point of view.

Establish which facts and issues all participants agree on and determine why different issues are important to each person. Identify common interests, which can be as simple as a mutual desire to resolve the problem without resorting to violence or a shared need to save face.

Take time to brainstorm about possible solutions to the problem.

Come up with a list of options without immediately judging them or feeling committed to them. Try to think of solutions where both parties gain something, think 'win-win' situation. Too often we assume that for one person to win, the other person has to lose. In reality, it is often possible to think creatively and come up with a solution that allows both people to feel good and walk away feeling that their needs have been met.

After a number of options are suggested, each person discusses his or her feelings about each of the proposed solutions. Participants will negotiate and need to compromise in order to reach a conclusion that is acceptable to both. They may need to agree to disagree about some issues to reach an understanding.

The persons involved will create a verbal agreement, or written agreement if participants feel it necessary, by explicitly stating the solutions agreed upon and the actions to be taken by each person. If necessary, set up a time to check back to see how the agreement is working.

The worst case scenario is when the parties involved are unable to come to an agreement. If all else fails, agree to disagree. It takes two people to keep an argument going. If a conflict resolution is going nowhere, you can choose to disengage and move on.

RELATIONS & REMEDIES

Let it go.

If we have a poor relationship with someone in the present, it can be the result of lingering anger or resentment from the past that of which we refuse to let go. This does not necessarily mean that the anger or resentment has not been expressed; we may have expressed those emotions and displeasure at the time, but are still holding on to those feelings.

After having a difficult encounter, it can be hard to let go of all the feelings, frustrations and residue of that episode in life. Before we become ready and able to face the next difficult situation or conflict with a clean slate, we have to let go of any repressed feelings, ideologies or unhelpful notions we hold.

Think of a past conflict with someone and try to see things from their perspective. How might you show this person that you understand his or her perspective, even though you do not agree?

Write down three questions that you could ask this person to show a desire to understand his or her interpretation of the topic or situation.

I.

_____

_____

_____

_____

_____

_____

EXERCISE

2.

_____

_____

_____

_____

_____

_____

3.

_____

_____

_____

_____

_____

_____

After filling out the above, make a decision about approaching this individual and trying to resolve this past conflict.

Forgive & Move On

It's one of the greatest gifts you can give yourself is to forgive.
I Maya Angelou

Forgiveness is defined as, "to pardon; to give up resentment of; to cease to feel resentment against." As we go through life, it is inevitable that we will come across people who wrong us in one way or another. Rather than focus our energy on influencing their behavior, we can learn to take better control over how we react to them.

Forgiveness is an act of giving. It can be costly because we are releasing someone from a debt in which they owe to us. True forgiveness can occur even when someone may not deserve to be pardoned. Our confidence always grows when we refuse to react to others and take the high road. Lack of forgiveness acts as a protective shield to keep further harm from occurring, but could possibly have the reverse effect of creating insecurities, making it harder for us to forgive future transgressions.

Choosing to carry a grudge forever keeps us from ever repairing the relationship, should it be worth repairing. Therefore, it is generally in our best interest to let go of the situation and pardon the offense. Long after we have forgotten what the other person actually did, we continue to focus our energy on being upset or angry with that person.

Most of the time we want and need to know that whoever caused us pain feels sorry for what they have done. We want them to admit that they did something wrong and acknowledge that they have hurt us. It is important that someone acknowledges their wrong-doing, however, we must still deal with the pain inflicted upon us, and letting go of this pain is where true forgiveness resides.

Practices to let go.

Empathy: Forgiveness is the recognition that people who harm others or say hurtful things are expressing their own unresolved pain and issues.

Meditation: Reflecting on the situation and finding internal insight can be a shortcut in the forgiveness process. Listen to your inner self talk to ensure that it reflects the true meaning of forgiveness.

Visualization: Visualize the person you have decided to forgive. Imagine that an energy cord connects you to the situation or person. Affirm back your energy, and unplug the cord, not allowing that person or the situation to drain you any longer.

Journal: Express your feelings to the person you are forgiving by writing a letter. Using your journal to write daily affirmations also helps in confirming your decision to forgive.

Patience: Forgiveness is an ongoing process; it is rarely completed on the first attempt.

Although it might seem like forgiveness is a benefit for someone else, it is actually a personal action for one's self. Understand that forgiveness does not involve approval of wrong-doing, instead it is a personal decision to move on from any pain caused.

Negative feelings, including pain, betrayal, frustration, guilt and fear, can debilitate and harmfully affect our confidence if left unresolved. The conscious act of forgiveness releases the negative feelings and frees us from suffering or allowing ourselves to dwell in the negativity.

THE
FORGIVE
EXERCISE

1. Call, see, or write to someone who wants your forgiveness, but is unsure that you have forgiven him or her.

2. Let this person know that you will no longer hold his or her actions against him and that you are forgiving him or her completely.

3. If you need forgiveness from this person in return, do not be afraid to ask for it.

4. If this step is too soon for you, then make a commitment to work to let go of the offense so that both of you can be freed up from this previous pain.

THE GIVE EXERCISE

Do a "give back to the world" activity. Here are some possible actions:

» Contribute a monetary donation or volunteer time to a local church or charity.

» Write a letter of encouragement for someone who is in need of uplifting.

» Call a relative who would love to hear from you.

» Do something special for a family member that is outside of the ordinary.

» Compliment a complete stranger (such as a waitress or customer service individual).

» Do an act of service for someone who you believe needs a helping hand (wash car, garden work, etc.).

In the end it does not matter what you do. What matters is that giving back becomes a part of your weekly, if not daily, routine. You and your confidence will grow from this great activity.

Confident Internal
Strategies

Finding Yourself

If you don't like something, change it. If you can't change it, change your attitude.
| Maya Angelou

The most important element to finding happiness and success is finding peace and purpose within ourselves. If our opinion of ourselves is healthy, we are much better equipped to face the challenges of the world. If we have low self-esteem in who we are and low confidence in our ability, it will be impossible to positively progress in life or accomplish any life goals. Our life purpose lies within us and no other person can validate or quantify our existence.

Finding our strengths is one of the best ways to improve energy and effectiveness. In the grand scheme, our strengths can more than compensate for our weaknesses. In building confidence, it is not enough to only identify our weaknesses or areas of improvements. In addition, we need to recognize and celebrate our strong skill sets to develop a realistic understanding of ourselves.

Defining our values gives us purpose, helping us to avoid aimlessly drifting along in life. We should make decisions based on our internal compass, not solely on our current circumstance or social pressures. By ignoring our internal instincts, we end up fulfilling other people's expectations instead of our own. Wasting the person you are by attempting to be someone else is living without core values, leaving us feeling exhausted and empty. In contrast, living a life in line with our core values brings purpose, direction and happiness.

Part of finding oneself is releasing past issues and behaviors. The best thing we can do is learn from the past and behave differently in the future. To that extent, we must forgive our former selves for being shy or not behaving confidently in the past.

Often we spend valuable time and energy kicking ourselves for time and opportunities lost as a consequence of being self-conscious. From this point moving forward, release all negative feelings of frustration for being a less than confident in past experiences.

It is also a common practice for a past acquaintance to attempt to impose old limits onto us. They attempt to throw shade at us due to past encounters and continue at attempts to define us as shy or lacking confidence. When such feeble attempts are made to put us down or shake our confidence, we must display our newfound self by immediately, yet politely, inform them that we have changed and grown into a more self-assured and assertive person.

Fear of the unknown.

Life inherently has many unknowns. Because of the capacity of the mind to imagine things in relation to fear, the fear of unknowns can be far more pervasive than any other emotions and thoughts. Every emotion, including fear, has its origin in thought. The fear of the unknown is nothing more than an internal and mental obstacle that curbs our ability to perform to the fullest in various walks of life.

Fear is always relative, meaning it does not exist by itself. When we understand the true nature of fear, whether we are afraid of something real or imaginary, we should realize that the fear is of our own creation. Since we are the original creators of the fear and its construct, fear can be unraveled, unmade and undone in the same way.

One way to unravel fear is to educate ourselves about the fear, collect evidence and learn about the realities or improbability in order to put us at ease. A fear of being trapped in an elevator with nobody around to help is a dramatic fear and seemingly beyond anyone's control. Once we understand the truth behind the emotion, the fear loses its grip.

We cannot get rid of something unless we recognize and understand from where it stems. Learning about the real risk and likelihood of this happening allows us a great deal of control over the fear and can start to diminish the fear altogether.

In most instances it is counter-intuitive to spend valuable time and energy contemplating what might happen or using the fear of the unknown to halt or hinder our progress. Every time we encounter an unfamiliar situation, fear manifests itself, and prevents us from taking action and making potentially life altering decisions.

Of course, we make provisions to ensure that the worst-case scenario in all situations does not happen. Or if the worst-case scenario should happen, we attempt to minimize the damaging effects. The finer distinction is the difference between taking action to prevent or minimize the worst-case scenario and wasting time worrying about something that might happen without us taking action either way. Avoid spending time worrying or fearing, and instead, take action to increase peace of mind.

CONFIDENT STRATEGIES

Fear of change.

Fear of change can be subtle, operating under the radar convincing us that it is there to protect us and keep us safe. Most often a fear of change is accompanied by feelings of insecurity, being lost or confused. However, a life without a change is not acceptable, often becoming monotonous and unexciting.

Life changes regardless of how hard we try to prevent it from altering in any way. Much of the change we experience comes as a result of powerful and often painful transitions that can ultimately be of great benefit to us. We should always continue to evolve and grow which is always preferable to the alternative of life stagnation. We fear change, not because we love our current positioning, but because we dread altering behaviors or habits that seem to keep us afloat and surviving in life.

People are habitual creatures and normally do the same things repeatedly. This can be good in some contexts as it simplifies our lives so we do not have to consciously think about completing daily tasks such as driving a car, opening a door, or using a computer. On the flip side, this can be detrimental to our well-being if we act too much out of habit and become automatons, we lose our conscious choice for what we really want to do.

Being confident is a change that people may fear since becoming confident has an entirely new set of behaviors, attitudes, and values that differ from being shy or timid. Change is a useful benefit that should symbolize personal and professional growth, showing that we are not stagnate in life. On the outset, change may seem painful or have negative effects. We must always look on the bright side and think long-term on how this can help us.

Fear of failure.

We all have different definitions of failure simply because we all have different values and belief systems. A failure to one person might simply be a learning experience for someone else. It is impossible to go through life without experiencing some kind of failure or shortcoming. Truly confident people do not know for sure they will succeed at everything, but do know how to handle failure if it happens.

Fear of failure is closely linked to the fear of rejection and criticism, which leads us into patterns of procrastination and excuse making. When we are afraid of judgement from our failures, this can lead us to create an excuse to do nothing, no matter how potentially valuable and rewarding the experience.

When we focus on the things that could go wrong, we begin to picture all sorts of unlikely hypothetical situations, eventually talking ourselves out of doing what is in our hearts to achieve.

A fear of failure can also be a fear of failure *after success* which makes some people dwell on what will happen if or when we eventually fail. People in this frame of mind envision their success, but only see the ways in which they will disappoint people, their inability to handle the success gained, or the ways in which they will ultimately mess up their success. It is the fear of falling from the height of our success that can leave us reluctant to try in the first place.

When we venture outside our comfort zones, we need to focus on the potential benefits and remember why it is important to reach our destination. There is no such thing as failure; there are only results. Some results are better than others. If we encounter results that we do not like, we naturally adjust behaviors and strategies based upon those results while continuing our attempts at achieving our outcome.

Keep an open mind and think in terms of 'feedback' and 'results'. Rather than defining an experience as a success or failure, pay close attention to the results, which is the element that should be objectively considered. Remember that mistakes and mishaps are the way in which we learn. The more of them we make, the stronger the learning curve and ability to avoid the catastrophic ones that may occur. Without making mistakes, there is no personal growth, and with the absence of growth, there is only stagnation.

Change and goals go hand in hand. Think of something you would like to change about yourself internally or externally; mentally, physically or socially.

For instance, changing self-talk by reframing thoughts, losing weight by becoming more active, or boost confidence by improving grades. All of these changes would be the results of setting goals.

EXERCISE

Mental (this includes self-talk, confidence, self-esteem, negative/ intrusive thoughts, etc.)

What mental change would you like to see in yourself?

_____

_____

_____

_____

_____

_____

_____

_____

_____

_____

_____

EXERCISE

Why?

_____

_____

_____

_____

_____

_____

_____

_____

_____

_____

_____

_____

_____

_____

How will you make this change?

_____

_____

_____

_____

_____

_____

_____

_____

_____

_____

_____

_____

_____

_____

_____

State the Goal: (Be specific, make it measurable, attainable, realistic and time sensitive.)

_____

_____

_____

_____

_____

_____

_____

_____

_____

_____

_____

_____

_____

EXERCISE

Physical (this includes becoming more active, improved appearance, health, or performance in sports/exercise, etc.)

What physical change would you like to see in yourself?

_____

_____

_____

_____

_____

_____

_____

_____

_____

_____

_____

_____

EXERCISE

Why?

_____

_____

_____

_____

_____

_____

_____

_____

_____

_____

_____

_____

_____

_____

How will you make this change?

_____

_____

_____

_____

_____

_____

_____

_____

_____

_____

_____

_____

_____

_____

EXERCISE

State the Goal: (Be specific, make it measurable, attainable, realistic and time sensitive).

_____

_____

_____

_____

_____

_____

_____

_____

_____

_____

_____

_____

Social (this includes being a better friend, cooperating better with others, showing empathy, learning to accept constructive criticism, etc.)

What social change would you like to see in yourself?

_____

_____

_____

_____

_____

_____

_____

_____

_____

_____

_____

_____

Why?

_____

_____

_____

_____

_____

_____

_____

_____

_____

_____

_____

_____

_____

_____

_____

How will you make this change?

_____

_____

_____

_____

_____

_____

_____

_____

_____

_____

_____

_____

_____

_____

State the Goal: (Be specific, make it measurable, attainable, realistic and time sensitive).

_____

_____

_____

_____

_____

_____

_____

_____

_____

_____

_____

_____

EXERCISE

Fear of
Accomplishment

While one person hesitates because he feels
inferior, the other is busy making mistakes
and becoming superior.
| Henry C. Link

Fear of accomplishment may sound like a strange idea, but it is one in which many people can identify. In this scenario, a person adopts distance from success rather than putting it in the closest range possible. Even with a strong desire to succeed, many times we hold ourselves back by adding unnecessary difficulty and pressure to achieve our goals.

We may even approach our goals in a way that continues to create the same unsuccessful results. The unknown path that comes after our success may lead us to subconsciously create circumstances that keep us stuck. A fear of accomplishment can be described as an apprehension of being recognized or honored for our achievements, while also holding the belief that once we have made an achievement, we will not be happy or satisfied with the outcome.

Fear of achievement can also include:

»   Belief we are undeserving of the
    recognition that comes our way as
    a result of our accomplishments and
    successes.

»   Lack of belief in our ability to sustain our
    progression and the accomplishments we
    have achieved in life.

»   Fear that our accomplishments will self-
    destruct.

»   Belief that no matter how much we are
    able to achieve, there will never be long
    lasting success.

»   Belief that there are others out there
    who are better than us, who will replace
    or displace us if we do not maintain our
    performance record.

»   Belief that success is an end in itself;
    yet that end is not enough to sustain our
    interest and/or commitment.

»   Fear that once we have achieved the
    goals we have worked diligently for, the
    motivation to succeed will fade.

»   Fear that we will find no happiness in
    our accomplishments and be overall
    dissatisfied with life.

Some people fear success so much it can become paralyzing. Many people labor under the delusion that if one becomes successful that they have to move to a different neighborhood, possibly lose friends, or have to change who they are as individuals.

Other people shun success because they think the standards will be set too high and consequently, there will be additional pressure to perform consistently at that high level. We should always expect excellence from ourselves. We deserve to perform at a high level no matter what the context. We should always keep this in mind.

A fear of success can be dangerous because we can lose the motivation or the desire to achieve and grow. People overtaken by this type of fear can go as denouncing their accomplishments, seeking ways in which they can denigrate themselves to lose what has been gained.

Causes to fear
of success.

Fear of making foes.

Underlying a fear of success, there may be a fear of collecting enemies because of our success. Becoming successful changes how people perceive us, even if we have not changed as individuals. It can cause others to become envious and jealous because of our success. This fear becomes present because of an irrational idea that "people will hate me if I am successful". If this happens to be the case, it becomes an opportunity to weed out false friends making room to better cherish the real ones who remain. There will always be people who will respect us because of the feat that we were able to accomplish.

Fear of loneliness and isolation.

Loneliness is a feeling of being disconnected and alienated from others, making it difficult to have any form of meaningful contact. It is an emotional state in which a person experiences a feeling of emptiness and isolation. The fear of being alone can make us feel insecure, anxious and depressed.

An excessive fear of being alone may lead us to become overly needy of others people, ultimately allowing this need to control our lives. This fear can also lead us to think that when we succeed, we will become a different person that our friends will not accept and ultimately end up losing them and being alone. This is another irrational idea about fear and success.

Fear of spotlight and attention.

We all value our privacy, however, to attain a certain level of success we cannot be over-protective of our privacy. At a certain point, we will have to give up a portion of that privacy we enjoy to progress and get noticed if we want to be successful. Some of us also fear success because we do not want to be different or lose social approval.

We may also fear being in the spotlight because a lack of self-confidence. We may think that it is better for us to stay unnoticed rather than exposing ourselves to others. It is important to remember that success does not blend in with the rest of the crowd.

Fear of change.

Fear of change is the fear of moving outside the comfort zone we are used to occupying. Stepping outside the comfort zone is the only way to acquire new skills, learn new concepts, and apply these in real life, practical ways to acquire success. If we have the fear of change, then we may fear success also, as success is one of the things that will bring many changes into our life.

Ask yourself, what will happen when I succeed? What will change for the better? What will change for the worst? By confronting our fears, we take away their power. We are able to identify strategies for moving beyond them.

CONFIDENT STRATEGIES

Self-sabotage.

Self-sabotage is when our behavior or the actions we take create both short and long term problems and as a result, these distractions ultimately interfere with our desired goals. Common methods of self-sabotaging behaviors can range from procrastination to more serious and detrimental acts such as self-medication with drugs or alcohol, comfort eating, and forms of self-injury such as cutting. These acts may seem helpful in the moment, but ultimately undermine us, especially when we engage in them repeatedly.

Partying and partaking the night before.

We sabotage ourselves by not preparing or getting a good night's rest before an important event such as a big presentation, exam, or job interview. Also we might party literally (watching TV or dancing to music) or metaphorically (house cleaning until 3 am, drinking coffee or sugary drinks) to avoid thinking of and preparing for the task ahead of us.

It is important in our overall daily lives to manage and maintain a healthy diet as well as implement a proper sleep regime that allows us to be fully rested, restored and physically prepared for our big day. A healthy diet includes but is not limited to drinking plenty of water throughout the day, having 2-3 daily serving of fruits and vegetables and limiting the amount of processed foods, candies and sugar infused items we intake.

Procrastination.

A lack of confidence causes us to procrastinate because we are fearful of our inability to complete a task. The fear can be real and there may be a lack of skills, but sometimes it is a perception we have created in our minds and as a result, we may avoid the task completely. If we are truly lacking in skill to achieve a goal, it is important to research and find the information needed, ask questions and seek out training to improve upon ourselves and skill sets.

Procrastination includes putting off projects, assignments or other important work while we instead use our time to daydream or allow ourselves to be easily distracted with unnecessary chores and activities. Procrastination is a habitual behavior and cycle of self-doubt that we need to put our best efforts into breaking.

Keeping a list of the things we need to accomplish, including both long and short term goals, can help with procrastination. It is also important to reward ourselves for each item we have completed and are able to cross off the list. It is not easy to break old habits, but it can be done, and soon we will find that the new behavior becomes second nature.

All talk, no action.

Constantly talking about our life dreams and goals, while spending our nights watching TV and days randomly surfing the internet, rather than taking practical steps to move toward our goals is a waste of time and energy. We can build confidence by maintaining a high level of trust in our abilities. We have to consistently follow through with the tasks we assign to ourselves on a daily basis without exception.

Not taking action may look like laziness, but it is most likely self-sabotage, revealing a fear of success. Even on those days where it seems as though we are running on fumes, we have to push harder to boost our motivation and get something started. Nothing adds more value and belief in oneself as the transformation into an efficient and highly self-driven person.

The power of imagination has the ability to motivate us and help us to avoid the common pitfall of becoming stuck. We should create an image of the confident and self-assured person we aspire to become.

Negative self-talk.

Due to negative self-talk and what we assume people may think of us, we make lackluster attempts at opportunities because of the fear of how we will be received and the perception of others. To our disadvantage, we focus on what could go wrong instead of taking advantage of the chance we have in front of us. With negative self-talk, we may say things such as, *what is the use of preparing for the job interview? I probably won't get it anyway.* This is an example of self-sabotaging behavior that gives us an excuse for not doing our best.

Stop comparing yourself to other people. Low confidence and self-esteem stem from the feeling of being inferior by elevating others into a state of superiority. It is important not to be overly concerned or intensely focused on your neighbor, trying to keep up with their lives and what they are doing.

It will always serve us more to follow our own path, at our own pace rather than wasting time making comparisons.

Ways to overcome fear.

Mental preparation.

Mental preparation is one of the most important aspects before a big event, performance or moment in life. Some people make the decision to not only imagine themselves succeeding but also allow the possibility of failure to exist.

Sometimes when we picture the best case scenario of success and worst case scenario of possible embarrassment, we eliminate a lot of the pressure that naturally comes with important life events and that causes us to self-sabotage. By doing this, we instill confidence in our abilities to perform at our best.

CONFIDENT STRATEGIES

Face fears head on.

The purpose behind fear is to keep us safe and away from taking risks that are too dangerous. Though for many people, the power of fear keeps us from improving and progressing. In order to become confident we must believe change can be good by bringing us success and satisfaction in life.

Facing our fears is essential to living life to the fullest. We must explore the emotions we have about success and analyze what it is we really fear. This will allow us to think of ways to help in subsiding the emotion of fear, and over time it will gradually lose its impact.

Focus on the process.

It is important to gain clarity in life and invest in the areas that need the most attention and improvement. For example, if you find your finances in constant disarray, this is an important area in which to dedicate your attention. Organize and plan in order to make this part of your life more stable.

The more we build up each area of our life, the higher our overall esteem and confidence will grow. The end result may be important, but as with any journey, the individual steps can be more meaningful than the destination. We can concentrate on what we learn, the people we meet, and the experiences we collect as we move closer to our goal.

Analyze past successes.

Nothing is a stronger indicator of success than a past experience of success. With this experience intact, we have proof that something similar can be achieved because it has happened before. Subsequently this becomes a cycle, revealing to us that the more success we experience, the more confident we will become. With this added confidence, we are driven further to succeed and crave the experience and feeling of accomplishment.

Reflect on past projects and achievements; what obstacles did you face? How did success make you feel? What changed in your life as a result? This activity will help us clarify our abilities and overcome our fears.

Select worthwhile goals.

If we want to be successful in life, we should choose goals that are realistic and align with the path in which we desire to travel. We are all unique individuals, and our goals and journeys through life should reflect that dynamic. If we want success in life, our goals should be congruent with our values, strengths, passions and desired lifestyle.

Pursue goals that address your needs, not the needs of anyone else. Take the time to think through what success will really mean before making a commitment. We only need to be excited about success if it is what we truly desire.

Think about the rewards.

Rewards stimulate a positive cycle of change, especially when we get stuck in a mental rut. To create new paths or habits through a system of rewards, think of rewards as the fuel to keep us on track. When we celebrate a change in behavior with rewards, we are recognizing achievement, self-motivating and building confidence.

This last part is also key in order to maintain and improve our self-esteem, giving us the courage to keep moving forward. High esteem can counter inadequate feelings that may accompany a backslide into bad habits.

Do not let concerns about the future distract you from the positive benefits of reaching your goals. Visualize the upside: the final product, a satisfied customer, a check, or some other tangible result.

Be realistic.

Realistic feelings of confidence and positive self-esteem affect how we look, think and act, how we feel about others, and how successful we are in life. Having self-confidence does not mean that we can do everything. Confident people have expectations that are realistic. Even when some of their expectations are not met, they continue to be positive and to accept themselves.

It is also important to note that success will not solve all our problems, but the feeling of accomplishment can make everyday fears, stressors or irritations easier to work through and tolerate.

Create new behaviors.

After we start to discover the issues that hinder us and stunt our growth, we can start to devise new and creative strategies for moving forward. To decrease and gradually eliminate our fears, we can do something as simple as asking questions when we are unfamiliar or ignorant of a topic or situation. Not only does this demonstrate our interest in learning and growing, it also shows we have enough confidence in ourselves to acknowledge we do not know everything.

Important questions to ask oneself include: *How can I reinforce my self-confidence? What excuses or behaviors do I need to eliminate? How can I sustain my motivation?* Once we have these answers coupled with the strong will, determination and strategy, we will find the process of changing our behaviors to be less stressful and more attainable than our initial perception.

Write one feared action or activity on each sticky note. These can be work, school or home related. Keep writing these and tearing them off until you have run out of things that you have been avoiding.

Start putting them in order in terms of their impact on your confidence. For example, you might be avoiding asking a family member to change a behavior at home and might also be avoiding calling a former friend who is upset with you. Which of these has more of a negative impact on your confidence? Order them accordingly.

Now take off any sticky notes that represent things that you really should avoid because you objectively know that facing them would be more destructive than helpful (but make sure you are honest with yourself about this).

You should now be left with a few items that, due to your avoidance, are keeping your confidence from being at the highest level possible.

Now, pick one activity from the list you've made, and form a plan of attack by answering the questions below about it:

1. What do I need to do to overcome my fear of this action?

_____

_____

_____

_____

_____

_____

_____

_____

_____

EXERCISE

2. How will it benefit me to face this fear?

_____

_____

_____

_____

_____

_____

_____

_____

_____

_____

_____

_____

_____

3. How will it hurt me to avoid this fear?

_____

_____

_____

_____

_____

_____

_____

_____

_____

_____

_____

_____

_____

_____

_____

4. What action do I need to take with this (break it down into a smaller initial step if needed)?

_____

_____

_____

_____

_____

_____

_____

_____

_____

_____

_____

_____

EXERCISE

5. When will I do it?

_____

_____

_____

_____

_____

_____

_____

_____

_____

_____

_____

_____

_____

_____

Rebuilding Confidence

To wish you were someone else is to waste
the person that you are.
| Anonymous

Learning how to rebuild and maintain our confidence is essential to having a fulfilling life. Even the smallest achievement can be significant to start the process of rebuilding confidence and regaining self-esteem. There will always be situations that arise that make us question our abilities. Success, like failure, can become a habit. In our darkest moments when failure seems inevitable, the ability to take control and find success is more than possible with the right plan.

To sow a seed of confidence, there must be thoughtful yet simple, seamless planning, paired with commitment and motivation to see the task of building through to the end. Life is all about change, both big and small; epic and unseen; incredible and terrifying. Confidence crumbles when we start to reinforce feelings of uncertainty and insecurity. The more we believe in those empty feelings, the harder it becomes to go through life confidently.

A false self-image, especially one of perfection, can also cause a lack of confidence and low self- esteem. When we project a false image of who we want to be or how we want others to see us instead of who we really are, we not only lie to others, we perpetuate a lie to ourselves. The mind typically makes a comparison between the projected false image and the way in which we realistically view ourselves. The results of such a comparison can lead to harsh judgments, self-rejection, and feeling unworthy for not meeting the false image.

While the image of perfection appears to be a way for us to feel good about ourselves, in reality it causes us to reject ourselves and our strengths, creating feelings of unworthiness or 'not being good enough.' To eliminate this mental block, we must first dissolve the belief that we should fit into a mode of perfection, and embrace our positive attributes while working to strengthen our weakness.

When we change the way we feel about our shortcomings, while also recognizing our strong skill sets, we change the negative emotion attached to the mistake. Rebuilding confidence includes dissolving the belief is that we are inadequate. Beliefs such as these create emotions of insecurity and fear.

Changing beliefs of unworthiness and inadequacy includes recognizing that we are the ones making the judgment and observation of our "self" image. The criticisms are not coming from an outside source, but from within. Essentially, we are getting in our own way and allowing our minds to play tricks on us. Having this awareness helps us to realize we are the initial culprit of these beliefs and negative emotions. After this recognition, we can begin to shift our point of view and begin the process of changing how we view ourselves and abilities, appreciating who we are and nurturing who we will become.

Take Inventory.

To take inventory, we should create a mental or written list of our strong suits; talents and achievements, including personal, business or academic. This does not refer to material possessions. What are our intangible assets?

Ask questions such as:

» Am I healthy and free of serious ailments or disease?

» Do I have talents and capabilities that allow me to stand out and express myself?

» Do I have family and friends that support me?

No one is a carbon copy of the next; meaning that each one of us is inherently unique. Too often, we compare ourselves to other people. Recognizing our uniqueness is a good way of boosting confidence and self-esteem.

We should take pride in the fact that no one is exactly like us; no one can think, walk, or talk in the exact same ways. We can get entangled in negative thinking and comparisons such as we are not as intelligent, not as beautiful, not as wealthy, etc. At times we can belittle who we are, devaluing what we already possess, instead giving unnecessary focus to what other people may possess. When we focus on what we contribute to the world, there can be no comparisons, envy or regret.

Sometimes, we are so intently focused on our disappointments and frustrations that we forget to realize that we have so much in which to be confident. We all have our moments of doubt, confusion and uncertainty. We all have setbacks and obstacles in which we must contend, but we should not allow them to undermine our confidence.

Mingle with positive people; end unhealthy relationships.

We all want to feel valuable to the world and people closest to us. Having supportive and engaged friends provide us this value and balance in life. There is a powerful energy being around supportive people. Make friends with people who give encouragement and see the good in circumstances, instead of finding ways to be negative and dismissive.

Align yourself with friends who have a sunny disposition; those who choose to laugh and enjoy life, and look at the glass as half full, instead of half empty. If the people in our inner circle leave us feeling emotionally drained after interacting with them or subject us to mental put downs, no matter how constant or subtle, these are destructive relationships and need to be removed from our lives.

Have a positive outlook; tap into your inner confidence.

Awareness of our self-sabotage and negative thoughts is the beginning phase of rebuilding. We should take time to self-reflect in order to recognize and release destructive behaviors and thought patterns. Even the smallest of positive change or improvement manifested in our lives is worth celebration. Wake up speaking encouraging words, even before getting out of bed.

Instead of complaining about what is wrong or what does not work in our lives, focus on what is good and what does work well. The Law of Attraction dictates to us that what we focus on and pursue in life, we will receive. Do not allow negative thoughts of any kind to dictate the flow of the day. If it helps, repeat positive affirmations out loud. Every day it will get easier and easier to build; eventually it will come to a point where we naturally wake up every morning with a more positive attitude.

Challenge yourself; try something new and bold.

When we make plans to try something new, we must follow through. Making a commitment to see a task through to the end is one of the most important and effective ways to build lasting confidence. Whether it is taking a technology class, talking to your long-time crush, cooking your first family meal or going somewhere in the world you have never been before, this will help us open up our minds to more possibilities and opportunities.

When we expand our limitations, our confidence in our abilities begins to grow and we begin to believe in the many number of things we can do and actually do well. By trying something new on a continual basis we can also lessen our fears and live a life with less barriers. This type of action builds upon itself until we eventually find our challenges becoming more bold and daring.

Ultimately, our self-pride and confidence will grow in the process.

Stop engaging in negative activities.

Self-sabotage is typically described as a combination of negative thoughts, feelings and self-defeating behaviors, caused by low self-esteem and a lack of confidence that creates unnecessary road blocks on the path to success.

When we consciously want to achieve something but subconsciously set up obstacles that ensure we do not reach our goal, it can be concluded that inner sabotage is the culprit. These behaviors can be subtle, but by learning to recognize them, we can begin to overcome them.

Nutrition and mental health are closely related. It is also important to take care and treat our minds and bodies well. Wellness is a balance of physical, mental, spiritual, social and emotional elements in life and making positive choices in these areas. What we eat can, and will, affect our weight, increase or reduce the risk of chronic medical conditions, present or future, determine our energy level and ultimately affect our self-confidence and self-esteem.

Stop mistreating the body with poor sleep, copious amounts of processed foods and no physical exercise. Instead, make a strong effort to go to bed at a decent time, prepare healthier meals and get the recommended 30 minutes of exercise every day. These things do affect our mood which in turn, affects our self-esteem. If we do not display self-value and a sense worth, then no one else will treat us accordingly.

Give confidence to others.

Believing in others allows them to gain confidence. We can inspire confidence in others by providing trust, honesty and respect; treating people in the way in which we want to be treated. Building confidence in another person may be something as simple as remembering and addressing them by name or giving encouragement or complimenting them on how they look or what they have recently accomplished.

We should take care to make sure our motives in supporting others are genuine and purposeful as to not make the person feel as though our words or actions are guided by a personal agenda or ulterior motive. Showing random acts of kindness, without requiring anything in return, will help to boost a confident mind-set in others and within ourselves.

Face your fears in small steps.

Fear has always been the great enemy of success. It often holds us back from venturing out of our comfort zones. The fear of facing that new task head on, can be both daunting and overwhelming. For example, if you a become nervous while in a social gathering, you might not be able to accomplish the simplest of objectives such as introducing yourself to others or asking that person you admire on a date. The fear of being shunned or rejected can make many of us feel unable to take that step forward.

We often do not recognize the impact fear has in our lives simply because we use words such as worry, nervousness, stress, shyness or anxiety to mask and describe the emotion. Fear is an emotion that overrides our ability to think critically, preventing us from moving towards our goals, ultimately making our overall quality of life worse.

No matter our approach to overcoming fears, there will still be some level of initial fear, which may be crippling inertia for many people. Since fear is a state of mind, it is only as powerful as its representation in our minds. In the case of fear, it only has any real impact on us if we expect a painful consequence and outcome.

So what do you do? Take small steps to diminish and conquer the fear. These steps include acts like just saying hello to people or engaging in more conversations with others via social media, i.e. Twitter, Facebook, Instagram, SnapChat, etc. Becoming more involved in conversations at school and work will help you exercise your conversational muscle and skill.

If we access the images and dialog of fear in our mind, we can change this content into something that supports and motivates us, gradually reducing the impact the fear once held. Identify your fear and make a plan with smaller steps you can take to gradually lessen your discomfort.

Small steps out of the comfort zone:

» Call a long lost friend or relative.

» Engage in a social media chat session.

» Attend an event; talk to at least five unfamiliar people.

Mid size steps out of the comfort zone:

» Speak in front of a small group about a passionate subject.

» Volunteer at a not-for-profit to help others while building skills and comfort level.

Big steps out of the comfort zone:

» Quit your full time, safe, job to start your dream career.

Step out the comfort zone.

Fear of failure is what restricts us to our comfort zone, crippling our curiosity and discouraging us from taking risks. We fear going for what we want because we may fail, but by allowing our fears to control our destiny we have already failed. Our comfort zone is comfortable because it is where we know what to expect. Comfort zones vary in each area within our lives and can be a set of people, places or things in which we share a level of comfort.

A comfort zone is an invisible line we draw for ourselves to separate the things we feel are uncomfortable. Some people may feel very comfortable speaking in front of a large audience or even being on camera, yet they get cold feet when it comes to speaking with one person in particular.

We all have those invisible barriers – there is always something out there we seem to be reluctant to try. Our challenge is to perpetually expand this comfort zone, doing new and different things. By doing this we are allowing ourselves to evolve and grow.

Expect to achieve great things.

Research has shown that our expectations of being successful is a great predictor of our actual success with a particular task or challenge. It is also strongly believed that we can be proactive in our viewpoints or deeply held beliefs about ourselves. These viewpoints and beliefs can impact our lives, therefore outcomes are not controlled by external factors alone.

Many people underestimate how important it is to maintain an optimistic vantage point, and how, more often than not, a negative view will impact your performance and lead you to do less than your best. To keep everything in perspective, it is not a matter of allowing self-doubt in; this will happen to the best and most confident people. The problem is allowing self-doubt and opposition to success linger around in your mind. In essence, you begin to "psych yourself out".

**People with self-confidence who
adopt an optimistic attitude:**

» Tend to have a strong persistent attitude
when facing challenges.

» Put forth greater effort tasks.

» Have lower stress levels and a greater
peace of mind.

» Expect positive outcomes.

» Interpret challenges in life as obstacles
to overcome.

» Recover faster after failures.

REBUILDING CONFIDENCE

We can all recall childhood cartoons, stories or movies of our favorite characters fighting through some sort of challenge or adversity. In the end, they always persevere and achieve their objective. When they are at their lowest point in the story, they usually undergo some sort of change in attitude, or a greater sense of expectation that leads them to try again until they obtain the desired results. It is important we adopt the same mental toughness and resilience when it seems as though our tank is on empty and we have given it our all, we have to give it the last big push.

REBUILDING CONFIDENCE EXERCISE

We all have a unique purpose that we alone can fulfill. Follow the pattern below to work out your life's purpose. Reflect on your purpose and allow this knowledge to boost your confidence and self-esteem.

1. List 2 personal qualities that make you unique. For example compassionate and selfless.

_____

_____

_____

_____

_____

_____

_____

_____

_____

_____

_____

_____

_____

EXERCISE

Confidence Your Secret Weapon

2. List a couple of ways you like to express those qualities when interacting with other people. For example to inspire and to teach.

_____

_____

_____

_____

_____

_____

_____

_____

_____

_____

_____

_____

EXERCISE

3. Now imagine what your perfect life and world would look like. For example: Everyone is confident in themselves and achieving their goals or everyone is expressing love and supporting each other.

_____

_____

_____

_____

_____

_____

_____

_____

_____

_____

_____

_____

EXERCISE

4. Now combine everything in steps 1, 2 and 3 to create your purpose statement. For example: My purpose in life is to use my compassionate and selfless nature to inspire and teach others to be confident in themselves and achieve their goals, while expressing love and support to those around them.

_____

_____

_____

_____

_____

_____

_____

_____

_____

_____

Conclusion

A journey of a thousand miles begins with
a single step.
| Lao Tzu

The most important thing that I would like you take away from this guide is that we have to ability to change our circumstances in life. We have the ability to improve upon who we are in order to excel and reach the goals we say we want to achieve. We do not have to live with constant anxiety or being timid or anxious. With a healthy attitude, positive mindset and confident strategy in hand, we can run toward our goals knowing that they are attainable.

It is important to understand that our confidence is an essential fiber when building a strong foundation in life. We should work daily to develop a healthy mindset, free of unwanted and negative thought patterns. Any constant stressors or unproductive self-talk is only a hindrance and serves no benefit to us.

When we experience an uncomfortable situation where our confidence waivers or we do not react or respond in a confident manner, it is imperative to take away the lesson in the mishap but not to let it define us.

The main difference between those people who pursue their goals in life and those people who are seemingly stuck is the belief and trust they hold in their abilities and skills. Rebuilding our confidence after it has been bruised is a difficult challenge within itself and can leave us starting from scratch. Do not lose hope when this happens.

Be patient in this process, as it is a life long, continuous journey. There is no final point of arrival, only continual growth and change for the better. Every small step you take on a daily basis adds to your overall progression, putting you closer in reach to your goals. Expect great things to happen in your life and dedicate your time and energy into making your dreams a reality.

This guide only works when you decide to put the techniques presented into practice. Confidence has to be a habitual practice and the methods presented in this book should be used to benefit your life experiences and assist in your personal growth. The techniques covered are ones I have successfully used to transform my life from that of shy and unsure, into that of a confident woman who speaks with assurance.

I applaud you for taking the time to finish this book. The time and energy you have spent in receiving the messages and advice presented in these pages constitutes as an investment in your potential growth. Whenever you feel off track or need a refresher, this guide is will help you to regain focus.

May all your goals come true. Good luck to you.